Sept 3, 1970

75-4/71

C + Hv

POET'S HANDBOOK

923 Places to Send Poems

compiled and written

by JEANNE HOLLYFIELD

FIRST EDITION

Published by
Young Publications, Appalachia, Virginia 24216

Printed in the United States of America

Standard Book Number 911666-02-8

CONTENTS

POET'S

HANDBOOK

AN EDITOR SPEAKS OUT

by

Jeanne Hollyfield

"A poem begins with a lump in the throat," said Robert Frost. But he neglected to emphasize the disturbing fact that it usually ends with a rejection slip.

If you would have your poems appear in print, three things are essential. First, you must know how to write a poem. Second, you must know where to submit it for publication. And third, you must know the proper form to use in submitting.

I won't attempt to tell you how to write a poem. Billions of words have been written and spoken on this subject. Yet no one has ever succeeded in telling anyone how to write a poem. John Keats summarized the solution to this problem quite thoroughly when he said, "If poetry comes not as naturally as leaves to a tree, it had better not come at all."

Assuming that you know how to write poems, and that you have written several of them, it is to be expected that you will want to share them with other people by having them appear in print. To accomplish this, you must learn which publishers might use your poems. The primary purpose of this booklet is to give you that information. It lists more than 900 places to send poems for possible publication. Some of these "markets" will pay you as much as $50 for one good poem. Some of them will pay for your poem by giving you copies of the publication in which your poem appears. Some of the smaller publishers cannot afford any payment at all.

The third important requisite to becoming a regularly published poet is knowledge of the proper form in which to submit your poems. This part of the process is easy to learn, but the number of poets who regard it as unimportant is astonishing. Let me assure you it IS important.

If you have read any of the writers' trade magazines or books on professional writing, you know that you should always TYPE your manuscript, double-spaced, on a clean 8 1/2 x 11 inch sheet of paper, using ONE SIDE of the paper only. You should type only one poem on a page. The author's name and address should appear in the upper left-hand corner of every sheet, and the number of lines in the poem should appear in the upper right-hand corner. You should always make and keep at least one carbon copy of every poem. You should enclose a self-addressed, stamped envelope (often called S.A.S.E.) for the return of your material, or for correspondence. Your outer envelope should be addressed to "Poetry Editor" unless you know the actual name of the editor who selects poems.

No doubt you have read time and again that the form described above is the proper one to use when submitting poems. But the writer never bothers to tell you just WHY these rules should be followed. Let's examine them individually in regard to their importance.

Why should your poems be typewritten rather than written in long-hand?

The answer to this one is simple: they are easier to read. An editor must read many poems before selecting the few that will be published. Easier reading means faster reading, which saves valuable time for the editor. The copysetter, too, appreciates copy that is not difficult to read. It increases his production and helps to eliminate errors in transcription.

This is the age of the typewriter. Most editors today will not attempt to read poems written in long-hand. And poems that are not read certainly have no chance of acceptance.

If you are unable to do your own typing, try to find someone in your neighborhood who will type your poems for you. If you are not personally acquainted with a competent typist, you might contact one locally by placing an ad in your community newspaper. Or you can hire the professional typists who advertise in writers' trade magazines such as THE WRITER, AUTHOR AND JOURNALIST, and WRITER'S DIGEST. Their fees are reasonable, and they are experienced in producing manuscripts that will gain editorial attention.

Why should your poems be double-spaced rather than single-spaced?

If having your poems typewritten makes them easier to read, then having them typed with double-spacing makes them almost twice as easy. Also, the double-spacing allows more room to edit in the event your poem requires editing. The copysetter, too, prefers double-spacing.

Why should the poems be typed on an 8 1/2 x 11 inch sheet of paper?

It is the standard size used in the literary and journalistic professions. Editors are accustomed to handling that size paper. The files and other facilities in their offices are designed for that size. Anything smaller or larger presents a storage or filing problem, and is likely to be disposed of without much consideration.

In actual practice, however, editors do receive poems scribbled on everything from paper bags to toilet tissue. Such submissions attract a certain amount of attention. But it is never favorable attention.

Why is neatness so important in presenting poems for publication?

Slovenly and carelessly prepared manuscripts offend the aesthetic sense of many editors. Be sure that the alphabetical characters on your typewriter strike bars are clean, and that your ribbon is not too well worn. Don't send carbon copies, mimeographed copies, or copies made on office copying machines. Send the original copy.

In addition to giving aesthetic offense, a poorly prepared manuscript identifies you as an amateur or novice who has not yet learned the rules. Editors know that ninety-nine percent of the material received from beginning writers is unsuitable for publication. For this reason, a manuscript that bears evidence of amateurism and carelessness will not be given the attention it may deserve.

Why is it more advantageous to type only one poem on a page instead of several?

More often than not, only one or two of the poems will be accepted while the others will be rejected. Or the editor might want to hold only one for further consideration, knowing that the others are definitely not his type of material. This situation can be confusing to the editor. He might decide to solve the problem by simply returning ALL the poems.

Why is it necessary to enclose a self-addressed, stamped envelope (S. A. S. E.)?

This may seem like an insignificant thing to the writer, but it is of paramount importance to the editor. Certainly it would not require a great amount of effort or expense for the editor to use one of his envelopes, one of his stamps, and ask his secretary to type your address on the envelope and mail your poems back to you. That would not be much trouble at all IF your poems were the only ones he received that day. But in all probability he received 100, or maybe 1, 000, poetry submissions on the same day that yours arrived. If the editor used his own postage to return poems to 100 individual writers, the postage alone would cost at least $6. 00 at current postal rates. If he returned 1, 000 poems, the cost would be $60. 00, not to mention the cost of envelopes and his secretary's time.

The necessity of enclosing a self-addressed, stamped envelope cannot be emphasized too strongly. Very few editors will return your manuscript unless the envelope is enclosed.

Normally, you should submit from five to ten poems in one mailing. Your outer envelope should be a regular business size (#10) which is available at any United States post office. Your return envelope should be of the same size, but should be folded twice to lessen the chances of mutilation in the process of opening. It is not necessary to enclose a letter to the editor stating that you are offering the poems for publication. He will know. If for some reason you feel that you should write to him, make your letter as brief as possible. Editors are busy people. They can't spare the time to read lengthy accounts about your personal life regardless how interesting a person you may be.

Why should you keep a carbon copy of every poem you submit for publication?

For practical reasons. There are many ways in which a manuscript can be lost or destroyed. Mail trucks sometimes wreck and burn. Airplanes crash and explode. Postal employees and editorial departments can misplace your poems. By keeping a carbon copy in your file or desk drawer, you can make another original copy for submission in the future.

Why should your name and address appear on every page of your poetry manuscript?

As stated previously, it is likely that the editor will select only one or two poems from a given sheaf. Later, when your selected poem is ready to be set in type, it will be included in a large group of poems written by many different authors. The editor needs your name on your poem to identify you as author of that particular poem. And he might need your address for correspondence at a later date.

Some other points on which you should be informed if you would improve your relationship with editors are these:

Unless you are submitting an entire book manuscript to a book publisher, send only a small number of poems. From five to ten should be sufficient. Large, bulky manuscripts discourage an editor. Unless some of the first ten poems appeal to him he won't read the others anyway.

Avoid the use of paper clips or staples. Don't use manuscript binders or cardboard stiffeners. Such paraphernalia are annoying to editors. They prefer a simple, unbound group of poems.

Don't type poems on both sides of a sheet. Paper is not that expensive, and some of the poems are apt to be overlooked.

Don't try to draw attention to yourself by mailing a new poem to the editor every day for several days. The editor will remember you all right—with disgust. It is a good practice to mail poems every day. But mail them in groups. And to different editors.

Don't send biographical material or pictures unless they are requested.

Be consistent in the use of your name as author. For example, if you are a female poet, don't use Mrs. John Smith on some of your material, then use Lou Ellen Smith on the rest. If you are a male poet, don't use John Smith on some poems, and J. H. Smith on others. This practice is confusing to editors, copysetters, file clerks, and mail room employees.

Pen names, too, are irksome. Don't adopt one unless you have a very special reason to do so.

Always check the spelling and grammar in your poems before sending them out. If you are not illiterate, why let yourself appear to be?

When you finish writing a poem, wait a few days before submitting it for publication. An idea that seems brilliant to you today might seem ludicrous tomorrow. At least you will be able to detect any minor flaws that might have passed unnoticed when the poem was first written. You can then correct these flaws, edit the poem yourself, and improve its chance of acceptance when read by an editor.

Try to familiarize yourself with any magazine to which you would like to submit poems. You should read at least one issue before submitting material for publication. You might find a copy on your local news stand or in your local book store. Or perhaps your public library will have the latest issue. If you can't find a copy of the magazine at either place, you can write to the publisher and ask the price of a sample copy. But be sure to enclose a self-addressed, stamped envelope. Otherwise, you might not get an answer. Don't ask for a free sample copy unless you know definitely that the magazine gives free copies to writers.

Let us assume that you have written a poem which you believe is worthy of publication. You have followed the recommended rules in submitting it, yet it is promptly rejected. Does that mean that the editor regarded it as lacking in literary merit?

No. There must be thousands of other reasons why your poem might be rejected. An editor whose son drowned last week will be unimpressed by a poem describing the beach at sunset. A lady editor who has been supporting a shiftless and unaffectionate husband for twenty years is not likely to care for poems about marital bliss. If your manuscript arrives on the morning after a night of excessive revelry, the intensity of the editor's hangover might have some bearing on his appreciation of your jolly sense of humor or your elated outlook on life.

Besides petty, personal prejudices and idiosyncrasies, there are many other reasons why your poem may not be accepted at a particular time. The editor might have printed a poem similar to yours in his latest issue. He might prefer traditional verse, while yours is avant garde. Or he might have already accepted enough good poems to make up several issues, and is simply not in the market at present.

The principal reason why many good poems are rejected today is that more good poems are being written than the poetry publishing media can use. A magazine that can publish only 200 poems per year might be offered as many as 5,000. Obviously, the remaining 4,800 must find a home elsewhere or remain unpublished.

The important thing is to keep your poems in circulation at all times. When rejected by one publication, send them to another. Don't be discouraged by rejection slips. All writers, both professional and amateur, receive their share of them. One professional poet said, "I think no more of a rejection slip coming in than I do of the weather report I hear only vaguely in the midst of a hurried breakfast." After all, the very nature of free-lance writing is speculative. If you really believe in yourself and in your poems, don't ever give up. Keep on writing. And submitting. Somewhere you will find an audience.

THE MARKET LIST

*ANIMAL MAGAZINES

CATS MAGAZINE, 4 Smithfield St. , Pittsburgh,
Pa. 15222. Pays 20¢ a line.

HORSEMEN'S JOURNAL, 425 13th St. N. W. ,
Suite 1038, Washington, D. C.

THE WESTERN HORSEMAN, 3850 North Nevada
Ave. , Colorado Springs, Colo. 80901. Pays $15
to $20 a poem.

*ASSOCIATION CLUB AND FRATERNAL
  MAGAZINES

THE AMERICAN LEGION MAGAZINE, 720
Fifth Ave. , New York, N. Y. 10019. Pays $2.50
a line.

THE LOOKOUT, Seamen's Church Institute, 15
State St. , N. Y. , N. Y. 10004. Pays $5.00 a
poem.

THE ROTARIAN, 1600 Ridge Ave. , Evanston,
Illinois 60201. Pays $1.00 a line.

THE VILLAGER, 135 Midland Ave. , Bronxville,
N. Y. 10708.

*BUSINESS AND FINANCE MAGAZINES

INVESTMENT SALES MONTHLY, 314 Minorca
Ave., Coral Gables, Fla. 33134. Pays $10.00 a
poem.

*CONFESSION MAGAZINES

TAN, 1820 S. Michigan Ave., Chicago, Ill. 60616.
Pays $5.00 a verse.

*DETECTIVE AND MYSTERY MAGAZINES

MYSTERY LOVER NEWSLETTER, P. O. Box
107, Revere, Mass. 02151. Pays on publication.

*FARMING AND RURAL INTEREST
 MAGAZINES

AMERICAN AGRICULTURIST, P. O. Box 370,
Ithaca, New York 14850. Pays $3.00 a poem.

FARMLAND, P. O. Box 7305, Kansas City, Mo.
64116. Pays $5.00 to $15.00 a poem.

THE FURROW, Deere & Co., John Deere Road,
Moline, Illinois 61265. Pays $1.00 a line.

PENNSYLVANIA FARMER, 2436 N. Second St.,
Box 3665, Harrisburg, Pa. 17105.

THE PROGRESSIVE FARMER, 821 North 19th
St., Birmingham, Ala. 35202. Payment varies.

THE RURAL NEW YORKER, P. O. Box 370,
Ithaca, New York 14850. Pays $3.00 a poem.

SUCCESSFUL FARMING, 1716 Locust St., Des
Moines, Iowa 50303. Pays $3 to $5 per poem.

*GENERAL EDITORIAL MAGAZINES

THE ATLANTIC, 8 Arlington St., Boston, Mass.
02116. Payment varies.

EYE, 542 La Guardia Pl., N. Y., N. Y. 10012

HARPER'S MAGAZINE, 2 Park Ave., Room 1809
New York, N. Y. 10016. Pays $2.00 a line.

LOOK, 488 Madison Ave., New York, N. Y.
10022. Pays $25.00 minimum a poem.

THE NEW YORKER, 25 W. 43rd St., New York,
N. Y. 10036. Payment varies.

PAGEANT, 205 E. 42nd St., N. Y., N. Y. 10017

*HEALTH AND MEDICINE MAGAZINES

LISTEN MAGAZINE, 6840 Eastern Ave. N. W.,
Washington, D. C. 20012. Payment varies.

*HI-FI AND MUSIC MAGAZINES

THE JUNIOR MAGAZINE, Baptist Sunday
School Board, 127 Ninth Ave. N. , Nashville,
Tenn. 37203. Payment varies.

*HISTORY MAGAZINES

BITS AND PIECES, Box 746, Newcastle, Wyo.
82701. Payment in contributors copy.

*HOME SERVICE AND GARDEN MAGAZINES

GOURMET, 777 Third Ave. , New York, N. Y.
Payment varies.

*HUMOR MAGAZINES

HUMORAMA, INC. , 136 E. 57th St. , New York,
N. Y. 10022. Pays 45¢ a line.

*JUVENILE AND YOUNG PEOPLE'S
   MAGAZINES

ACCENT ON YOUTH, 201 8th Ave. S. , Nashville, Tenn. 37203. Payment varies.

ADVENTURE, 127 Ninth Ave. North, Nashville,
Tenn. 37203

AMERICAN JUNIOR RED CROSS NEWS, % American National Red Cross, 18th and D Sts., Washington, D. C. 20006.

THE CHILDREN'S FRIEND, 79 S. State St., Salt Lake City, Utah 84111. Pays 25¢ a line.

CONQUEST, 6501 The Pasco, Kansas City, Mo. 64131. Pays 10¢ a line.

COUNTDOWN, St. Joseph Seminary, P. O. Box 245, Westmont, Illinois 60559.

FIVE/SIX, 201 8th Ave. S., Nashville, Tenn. 37203. Pays $1.00 a line.

FRIENDS, Warner Press, Box 2499, Anderson, Indiana 46011. Pays 15¢ a line.

GOD'S CHILDREN, Concordia Children's Newspapers, 3558 S. Jefferson Ave., St. Louis, Mo. 63118. Pays $2.00 a poem.

THE GOLDEN MAGAZINE, 850 Third Ave., N. Y., N. Y. 10022. Payment varies.

GUIDE, Pilgrim Publishing House, 230 East Ohio St., Indianapolis, Ind. 46204.

HAND IN HAND, Augsburg Publishing House, 426 S. 5th S., Minneapolis, Minn. 55415. Pays $5 to $15 a poem.

HIGH SCHOOL SIGNAL, Pilgrim Publishing

House, 230 East Ohio St., Indianapolis, Indiana 46204.

HIS PEOPLE, Concordia Children's Newspapers, 3558 S. Jefferson Ave., St. Louis, Mo. 63118. Pays $2.00 a poem.

HUMPTY DUMPTY'S MAGAZINE, 52 Vanderbilt Ave., N. Y., N. Y. 10017. Pays $10.00 a poem.

IMPACT, Board of Ed. and Publ., American Baptist Convention, Valley Forge, Pa. 19481. Payment varies.

JACK AND JILL, Independence Square, Philadelphia, Pa. 19105. Payment varies.

JOURNEYS, Church of the Brethren, 1451 Dundee Ave., Elgin, Illinois. Pays 5¢ a line.

JUNIOR CHALLENGE, 922 Montgomery Ave., Cleveland, Tenn. Pays 50¢ a poem.

JUNIOR DISCOVERIES, 6401 The Pasco, Kansas City, Mo. 64431. Pays 50¢ for each 4 lines.

JUNIOR MESSENGER, 722 Main St. Box 347, Newton, Kansas 67114. Pays 10¢ a line.

JUNIORS, American Baptist Board of Ed. and Publ., Valley Forge, Pa. 19481. Pays 25¢ a line.

JUNIOR WORLD, Box 179, St. Louis, Mo. 63166. Pays 25¢ a line.

THE KINDERGARTNER, 201 8th Ave. South, Nashville, Tenn. 37203. Pays $1.00 a line.

NURSERY DAYS, 201 8th Ave. South, Nashville, Tenn. 37203. Pays to $1.00 a line.

PACIFIC PRESS PUBLISHING ASSOC., 1350 Villa St., Mountain View, Calif.

OUR LITTLE MESSENGER, 38 West Fifth St., Dayton, Ohio 45424. Pays $5.00 a poem.

PURRING IN A POCKET, 3948 North 51st Blvd. Milwaukee, Wisc. 53216.

REACH, Warner Press, Anderson, Indiana 46011. Pays 15¢ a line.

SCOUTING MAGAZINE, Boy Scouts of America, New Brunswick, N. J. 08903. Pays $5 to $10 a poem.

SENIOR HI CHALLENGE, 922 Montgomery Ave. Cleveland, Tenn. 37311. Pays $1.00 a poem.

SEVENTEEN, 320 Park Ave., N. Y., N. Y. 10022.

STEPS, Augsburg Publishing House, 426 S. Fifth St., Minneapolis, Minn. 55415. Pays $5 to $10 a poem.

STORY FRIENDS, Mennonite Publ. House, Scottsdale, Pa. 15683. Pays 12 1/2 ¢ to 15¢ a line.

STORYLAND, Box 179, St. Louis, Mo. 63166.

STORYTIME, 127 Ninth Ave. North, Nashville, Tenn. 37203.

STORY TRAILS, Light and Life Press, Winona Lake, Indiana 46590. Pays 20¢ a line.

STORY WORLD, American Baptist Board of Ed. and Publ., Valley Forge, Pa. 19481. Pays 25¢ a line.

STRAIGHT, 8121 Hamilton Ave., Cincinnati, Ohio 45231. Payment varies.

SUNDAY SCHOOL EXTRA, 1816 Chestnut St., Philadelphia, Pa. 19103. Pays $1.00 a stanza.

SUNDAY SCHOOL MESSENGER, Pilgrim Publ. House, 230 East Ohio St., Indianapolis, Ind. 46204 Pays 10¢ a line.

TEENWAYS, Augsburg Publ. House, 426 S. 5th St., Minneapolis, Minn. 55415. Pays $5 to $10 a poem.

TELL ME, Church of the Brethren, 1451 Dundee Ave., Elgin, Illinois. Pays 5¢ a line.

THREE/FOUR, 201 8th Ave. South, Nashville, Tenn. 37203. Pays 50¢ to $1.00 a line.

UPWARD, 127 9th Ave. North, Nashville, Tenn. 37203. Pays 35¢ to 50¢ a line.

VENTURE, 910 Witherspoon Bldg., Philadelphia, Pa. 19107. Pays 25¢ a line.

VISION, P. O. Box 179, St. Louis, Mo. 63166. Pays 25¢ a line.

WEEKLY BIBLE READER, 8121 Hamilton Ave., Cincinnati, Ohio 45231. Pays $2 to $5 a poem.

WEE WISDOM, Lee's, Summit, Mo. Pays 25¢ a line.

WONDER TIME, 6401 Pasco, Kansas City, Mo., 64141. Pays 12 1/4 ¢ per line and up.

WORDS OF CHEER, 610 Walnut St., Scottdale, Pa. 15683. Pays 25¢ per line and up.

WORLD OVER, 426 W. 58th St., New York, N. Y. 10019. Pays $10 to $15 a poem.

YOUNG CATHOLIC MESSENGER, 38 West Fifth St., Dayton, Ohio 45402. Pays $5 and up a poem.

YOUNG EXPLORERS, Concordia Children's Newspapers, 3558 S. Jefferson Ave., St. Louis, Mo. 63118. Pays $2.00 a poem.

YOUNG HAWAII, 740 Ala Moana Blvd., Honolulu, Hawaii 96813.

*MILITARY MAGAZINES

LEATHERNECK, Headquarters, U. S. Marine Corps, P. O. Box 1918, Washington, D. C. Pays $10.00 a poem.

THE LINK, 122 Maryland Ave. N. E., Washington, D. C. 20002. Pays $1.00 a stanza.

*MISCELLANEOUS GENERAL MAGAZINES

ARCHAEOLOGY, 132 George St., Rutgers Univ., New Brunswick, N. J. 08903.

THE CRUCIBLE, Executive Office 1317, Box 354, Duluth, Minn. 55802.

HARVEST YEARS, 104 E. 40th St., New York, N. Y. 10016. Pays $5.00 a poem.

IDEALS, 11315 Watertown Plank Rd., Milwaukee, Wisc. 53225.

MATURE YEARS, 201 8th Ave. S., Nashville, Tenn. 37203. Pays 50¢ to $1.00 a line.

QUINTO LINGO, 33 E. Minor St., Emmaus, Pa. 18049.

QUOTE MAGAZINE, Droke House, Inc., P. O. Box 683, 1109 S. Main St., Anderson, S. C. 29621 Pays $1.00 a poem.

STUDENT, 220 Park Ave. South, N. Y., N. Y. 10003.

TODAY'S SPEECH, 121 Edgehill Rd., Syracuse, N. Y. 13224.

UNDERSTANDING MAGAZINE, P. O. Box 206, Merlin, Oregon 97532. Pays 10¢ a line.

*NATIONAL AND WORLD AFFAIRS
 MAGAZINES

COMMONWEAL, 232 Madison Ave., N. Y., N. Y. 10016.

THE MONORITY OF ONE, 155 Pennington Ave. Passaic, N. J. 07055.

NATIONAL REVIEW, 150 E. 35th St., New York, N. Y. 10016.

*NATURE MAGAZINES

NATIONAL WILDLIFE, 534 N. Broadway, Milwaukee, Wisc. 53202. Payment varies.

*NEGRO MAGAZINES

NEGRO DIGEST, 1820 S. Michigan Ave., Chicago, Illinois 60616. Pays $5 to $25 a poem.

*NEWSPAPERS AND SUNDAY SUPPLEMENTS

CHICAGO TRIBUNE MAGAZINE, 435 North
Michigan Ave., Chicago, Ill. 60611. Pays $10.00
and up.

THE CHRISTIAN SCIENCE MONITOR, 1 Nor-
way St., Boston, Mass. 02115. Pays $20 a poem.

SUBURBAN TIMES PUBL. CORP., 355 Washington St., Braintree, Mass. 02184.

THE NEW YORK TIMES MAGAZINE, Times
Square, N. Y., N. Y. 10036.

THE PHILADELPHIA EVENING AND SUNDAY
BULLETIN, 30th and Market Sts., Philadelphia,
Pa. 19101.

*POETRY MAGAZINES

THE AMERICAN BARD, 1154 N. Ogden Dr.,
Hollywood, Calif. 90046. Prizes.

AMERICAN POET, 830 7th St., Charleston, Ill.
61920.

ATLANTIS EDITIONS, 4910 N. 12th St., Philadelphia, Pa. 19141. Payment in contributors
copies.

BACHAET, 19 Dupont Pl., Irvinton, N.J. 07111

BARDIC ECHOES, 1036 Emerald Ave. N. E., Grand Rapids, Mich. 49503. Payment in contributors copies.

THE BELOIT POETRY JOURNAL, P. O. Box 2, Beloit, Wisc. 53511. Payment in copies.

BEST IN POETRY, 133 W. 6th St., Deer Park, N. Y. 11729. Pays 10¢ to $3.00 per poem.

BLACK SUN POETRY MAGAZINE, 70 Pierrepont St., Brooklyn, N. Y. 11201. Payment in contributors copy.

CAPE ROCK JOURNAL, Southeast Missouri State College, Cape Giradeau, Mo. 63701.

CARDINAL POETRY QUARTERLY, 10418 West Drummond Pl., Melrose Park, Ill. 60164. Annual awards.

CREATIVE REVIEW, 1718 S. Garrison, Carthage Missouri 64836. Payment in contributors copy.

CYCLOFLAME, 212 West First St., San Angelo, Texas 76901. Pays $1.00 a poem.

ELIZABETH, 103 Van Etten Blvd., New Rochelle New York 10804. Payment in contributors copies.

EPOS, Crescent City, Fla. 32012. Payment in four contributors copies.

ESSENCE, 91 Westerleigh Rd., New Haven, Conn. 06515. Payment in contributors copies.

THE GREEN WORLD, P. O. Drawer LW, University Station, Baton Rouge, La. 70803.

HAIKU HIGHLIGHTS, P. O. Box 15, Kanona, N. Y. 14856. Contests.

IMPRINTS QUARTERLY, 300 Peerson Ave., Newark, N. Y. 14513. Payment in contributors copy and awards.

JEAN'S JOURNAL OF POEMS, Box 15, Kanona, N. Y. 14856. Pays in cash prize awards.

KAURI, % Will Inman, P. O. Box 429, American University, Washington, D. C. 20016. Payment in contributors copy.

THE LYRIC, Bremo Bluff, Virginia. Payment in contributors copies and prizes.

MAINE SUNDAY TELEGRAM, "Poetpourri" Portland, Maine 04106. Pays $5 a poem.

MELE, Dept. of Euro. Lang., University of Hawaii, Honolulu, Hawaii 96822. Payment in contributors copies.

THE MUSE, Rt. 1, Box 301, Cathlamet, Wash. 98612.

NEW: AMERICAN & CANADIAN POETRY, John Gill, R. D. 3, Trumansburg, New York 14886. Payment in contributors copies.

OREGONIAN VERSE, The Oregonian, Portland, Oregon 97201. Pays $1.00 a poem.

ORPHIC LUTE, 3815 Mercier, Kansas City, Mo. Prizes.

PASQUE PETALS, Box 117, Valley Springs, S.D.

PERSONAL POETRY BROADCASTS, (Radio program) 110 Richards Ave., Winchester, Va. 22601 Pays in certificate & tapes.

PLIEGO, 6191 S. W. Capitol Highway, Portland, Oregon 97201. Payment in contributors copies.

PODIUM, 701 East Schaaf Rd., Brooklyn Heights, Ohio 44131. Payment in contributors copies.

POEM, P. O. Box 1247 West Station, Hunstville, Ala. 35807. Pays $5.00 a poem.

POET AND CRITIC, Dept of Engl., Iowa State University, Ames, Iowa 50010. $30.00 prize.

POET LORE, 36 Melrose St., Boston, Mass. 02116. Awards.

POETRY, 1018 N. State St., Chicago, Ill. 60610. Pays 50¢ a line.

THE POETRY BAG, 608 Missouri, Columbia, Mo. 65201. Payment in contributors copies.

POETRY FORUM, Denver Post, 615 15th St.,

Denver, Colorado 80202. Pays $2.00 a poem.

POETRY PARADE, 3295 Victory Center, North Hollywood, Calif. 91609. Cash & prizes.

POET'S BULLETIN, 8880 East Mexico Dr., Denver, Colorado 80222. Prizes.

POTPOURRI, 6191 S. W. Capitol Highway, Portland, Oregon 97201. Payment in contributors copies.

THE PRAIRIE POET, 830 7th St., Charleston, Illinois 61920.

QUOIN, 1226 W. Talmadge, Springfield, Mo., 65803.

SEVEN, 8 N. Broadway, Oklahoma City, Okla. 73102. Pays $3.00 a poem.

SOUTH AND WEST, 2601 S. Phoenix, Ft. Smith, Arkansas. Payment in contributors copy.

SOUTHERN POETRY REVIEW, Dept. of Engl., N. C. State University, Raleigh, N. C. 27607. Payment in contributors copies.

TANGENT, 9075 River Styx Rd., Rt. 2, Wadsworth, Ohio 44281. Payment in contributors copies.

UNITED POETS, 830 7th St., Charleston, Ill. 61920.

UNIVERSITY OF TAMPA POETRY REVIEW, University of Tampa, Tampa, Florida 33606. Payment in contributors copies.

WISCONSIN POETRY MAGAZINE, P. O. Box 187, Milwaukee, Wisc. 53201. Awards.

WORD, Department of English, University of Mexico, Albuquerque, New Mexico 87106. Payment in contributors copies.

ZIGGURAT, P. O. Box 88, Milwaukee, Wisc. 53201. Payment in contributors copies.

THE LITTLE MAGAZINES

This is the age of instant publishing. A used typewriter, a mimeograph machine, some manuscripts from friends, a few reams of paper in your bedroom or basement, and — presto! — you are a publisher!

Every year hundreds of so-called "little" magazines make their appearance in just this way. The publisher is also the editor, printer, office boy, secretary, copysetter, advertising manager, circulation manager, layout artist, and janitor.

Often it is a feeling of rebelliousness or frustration that prompts a person to undertake the publication of a little magazine. He might want to affirm his beliefs, expound his philosophies, or voice protest against the "establishment." In other cases, it is merely a quest for adventure, or a person's need to communicate with others whose interests are similar to his own. But the majority of little magazines are started by a person who has a passion for the new and experimental in literature, and wants to participate in its growth. He seeks only the gratification that comes with the knowledge of having published something of literary value, something which otherwise might have been lost to oblivion.

The publication of a little magazine is truly a labor of love. No rational-minded person would expect to make money from such a venture. As a rule, the magazines operate at a deficit. Not enough subscriptions and advertisements can be sold to compensate for the expenses incurred in publishing each issue. The deficit must be made up from money earned by the editor on his regular job, or by gifts from his friends and supporters. Sometimes an editor who is unusually dedicated to his project will take an extra job, or sell his automobile or furniture to raise money for publication. To a large extent, he substitutes labor for capital. One of the greatest and most admired of all little magazine publishers, Alan Swallow of Denver, literally worked himself to death publishing little magazines and small press books.

It should be noted, however, that not all the magazines of small circulation fit into the category described above. Some are sponsored and subsidized by colleges, universities, foundations, commercial printers, or bookstores. Many of them are artistically designed and handsomely printed on expensive, quality paper. But nearly all of them operate at a loss financially.

In spite of their limited circulation, the frequency with which they appear and disappear, and the crude form in which some of them are presented, the little magazines are extremely important to the literary scene. Their audiences are made up mostly of writers, students, and that fringe of society called Bohemia, but they are also read by commercial publishers, editors, and literary agents searching for new material. Many authors, now famous, were first published in the little magazines. Among them are: Ernest Hemmingway, William Faulkner, T. S. Eliot, Sherwood Anderson,

Allen Tate, Ezra Pound, William Carlos Williams, Norman Mailer, William Saroyan, Budd Schulberg, Truman Capote, John Cheever, Robert Penn Warren, Jesse Stuart, and Tennessee Williams.

You as a poet cannot afford to ignore the "littles." Without them, the amount of poetry published today would be meagre indeed. It is to your benefit that you read as many of them as possible. Submit your poems to them. Subscribe to them. And if you have something to sell, advertise in them. Their circulation is limited, but they are well-read. Nearly every subscriber reads every word in every issue—a fact often overlooked by many potential advertisers.

But don't think they will print just any material you send them. They are already receiving too many unpublishable poems. Your material must meet their standards of quality. But because they are so numerous and their interests so diverse, you should be able to gain acceptance in some of them if your poems contain any freshness in subject matter or form. You won't gain much in gold, but you will reap the satisfaction of having communicated with an audience of attentive listeners.

*LITERARY AND "LITTLE" MAGAZINES

ABYSS, 110 Margay St. , Dunkirk, N. Y. 14048
Payment in contributors copies.

THE ACTIVIST, 27 1/2 W. College, Oberlin,
Ohio 44074. Payment in contributors copies.

ALEDBARAN REVIEW, 2209 California St.
Berkeley, Calif. 94703. Payment in contributors
copies.

AMERICAN DIALOG, 32 Union Square, Room
804, New York, N. Y. 10003. Payment in contributors copies.

AMERICAN HAIKU, Box 73, Platteville, Wisc.
53818.

AMERICAN MERCURY, P. O. Box 1306, Torrance, Calif. 90505.

AMERICAN POET PRESS, Box 2182, Santa Fe,
New Mexico 87501. Payment in 12 copies, plus
half of profit, if any.

AMERICAN WEAVE, 23728 Glenhill Drive,
Cleveland, Ohio 44121. Payment varies.

ANALECTA, P. O. Box 133, Demarest, N. J.
07627. Payment in a years subscription.

ANGEL HOUR, 8635 Elm St. , Los Angeles, Ca.
90002. Awards.

ANN ARBOR REVIEW, 115 Allen Drive, Ann Arbor, Mich. 48103. Payment in contributors copies.

ANTE, P. O. Box 29915, Los Angeles, Calif. 90029. Payment $2.00 a poem.

ANTIOCH REVIEW, Antioch Press, Yellow Springs, Ohio 45387. Pays $5.00 per printed page.

ANUBIS, Golden Goblin Press, P. O. Box 323, Arlington, Va. 22210. Payment in contributors copies and cash as arranged up to 1¢ a word.

THE APPALACHIAN SOUTH, P. O. Box 4104, Charleston, West Virginia.

APPLE, P. O. Box 2271, Springfield, Illinois 62705. Payment in contributors copies.

APPROACHES, 110 South Maple, Elizabethtown, Ky. 42701.

THE ARCHER, P. O. Box 9488, North Hollywood, Calif. 91609. Payment in contributors copy.

ARION, 148 Waggener Hall, University of Texas, Austin, Texas 78712. Payment in contributors copies.

ARIZONA QUARTERLY, University of Arizona, Tucson, Ariz. 85721. Payment in contributors copies.

THE ARLINGTON QUARTERLY, University of Texas Press, Box 366, University Sta., Arlington, Texas 76010. Payment in contributors copies.

ARTS IN SOCIETY, 623 Extension, 432 N. Lake St., Madison, Wisc. 53706. Payment varies.

ARX, 12109 Bell Ave., Austin, Texas 78759.

ASPECTS, P. O. Box 3125, Eugene, Oregon 97403. Payment in contributors copies.

ATOM MIND, P. O. Box 827, Syracuse, N. Y. 13201.

AVALANCHE, Undermine Press, 2315A Russell St., Berkeley, Calif. 94705. Payment in contributors copies.

AWAKENER MAGAZINE, P. O. Box 1081, Berkeley, Calif. 94701.

BALL STATE UNIVERSITY FORUM, Ball State University, Muncie, Ind. 47306. Payment in contributors copies.

BELLA VISTA PRESS, 1110 Valley View Drive, Fayetteville, Arkansas 72701.

THE BENNINGTON REVIEW, Bennington College, Benn, Vermont 05201. Payment varies.

BEYOND BAROQUE, Box 675, Venice, Calif. 90291.

BITTERROOT, 5229 Utrecht Ave., Brooklyn, N. Y. 11219. Payment in contributors copies.

BLACKLIST, 44 Van Ness Ct., Maplewood, N. J. 07040. Payment in contributors copies.

BLUEBIRDS STAR, Box 86, Chenango Forks, N. Y. 13746.

BOKE PRESS, 40 Ave. B, Apt. 3B, New York, N. Y. 10009.

BOSS, Box 231, Village Station, New York, N. Y. 10014.

BRASS RING, Department of German, Fine Arts Building, University of Wisconsin-Milwaukee, Milwaukee, Wisconsin 53211. Payment in contributors copies.

BROADSIDE PRESS, 12651 Old Mill Rd., Detroit, Mich. 48238.

CALIFORNIA REVIEW, 280 E. Mountain Drive, Santa Barbara, Calif. 93103. Pays $2.00 per published page.

CAPTAIN FARLEY'S RAGWEED REVIEW, 4305 Drury Lane, Topeka, Kansas 66604. Payment in contributors copies.

CARLETON MISCELLANY, Carleton College, Northfield, Minn. 55057.

CAROLINA QUARTERLY, Box 1117, Chapel Hill, N. C. 27514. Pays $5.00 per poem, plus contributors copies.

CHALLENGE, 21002 Ave. San Luis, Woodland Hills, Calif. 91364. Payment in contributors copies.

CHARLATAN, St. Cloud State College, St. Cloud, Minn. 56301.

CHEER LETTER, 1706 Lee St., Houston, Texas 77026.

CHELSEA, Box 242, Old Chelsea Sta., New York, N. Y. 10011. Payment in contributors copies.

CHESHIRE MAGAZINE, 3058 N. Stowell, Univ. of Wisc., Milwaukee, Wisc. 53211.

CHICAGO REVIEW, University of Chicago, Chicago, Illinois 60637. Payment in contributors copies, plus 1 year sub.

CHOICE, P. O. Box 4858, Chicago, Ill. 60680. Payment in contributors copies.

CINQUEFOIL, 7626 Balfour St., Allen Park, Mich. 48101. Token payment plus contributors copy.

COLLEGE ENGLISH, National Council of Teachers of English., Wesleyan Univ., Middletown, Conn. 06457. Payment in contributors copies.

COLLEGE VOICE, Mercer Community College, 101 West State St. , Trenton, N. J. Payment in contributors copies.

COLORADO STATE REVIEW, 360 Liberal Arts, Colorado State University, Fort Collins, Colo. 80521. Payment in contributors copies.

CONCERNING POETRY, Department of English, Western Washington State College, Bellingham, Washington 98225. Payment in contributors copies.

CONFRONTATION, Long Island University, Greenvale, New York 11548. Pays $15 to $40 a poem.

CONGRESS, 160 Claremont Ave. , New York, N. Y. 10027. Payment in contributors copies.

CONSUMPTION, 4208 8th N. E. , Seattle, Wash. 98105. Payment in contributors copies.

COPKILLER, Box 2342, New Orleans, La. 70116. Payment in contributors copies.

COTTONWOOD REVIEW, Room 118, Kansas Union, Lawrence, Kansas 66044. Pays $1. 00 to $2. 50 a poem, plus contributors copies.

COUNTRY WORLD MAGAZINE, Rt. 2, Box 100, Carmi, Illinois 62821.

COYOTE BOOKS, 1562 Grant Ave. , San Francisco, Calif. 94133.

COYOTE'S JOURNAL, 1562 Grant Ave., San Francisco, Calif. 94133.

CRAZY HORSE, College of Arts & Sciences, NDSU, Fargo, North Dakota 58102. Payment in contributors copies.

CRONOPIOS, 138 S. 13th St., La Crosse, Wisc. 54601. Payment in contributors copies.

THE CRUCIBLE, Box 354, Duluth, Minn. 55801. Payment in contributors copies.

DASEIN, THE QUARTERLY REVIEW, G.P.O. Box 2121, New York, N.Y. 10001. Payment in contributors copies.

DECEMBER MAGAZINE, P.O. Box 274, Western Springs, Illinois 60558. Payment in contributors copies.

DEFINITION, 39 Grove St., New York, New York 10014.

DENVER QUARTERLY, University of Denver, Denver, Colorado 80210. Payment varies.

DESCANT, Department of English, Texas Christian University, Ft. Worth, Texas 77129. Payment in contributors copies.

DESERT REVIEW, 109 Washington Ave., Santa

Fe, New Mexico 87501.

DESPITE EVERYTHING, 1937 1/2 Russell St.,
Berkeley, Calif. 94703.

DIMENSION, 11 Bittersweet Circle, Penfield,
N. Y. 14526. Payment in contributors copies.

DION, 4032 W. Century Blvd., Inglewood, Calif.
90304. Payment in contributors copies.

DISCOURSE, Concordia College, Moorhead,
Minn. 56560. Payment in contributors copies.

DISCUSSION, P. O. Box 925, Millen, Georgia
30442.

DO-IT !, 1137 Hayden, Collenwood, Cleveland,
Ohio 44110. Payment in contributors copies.

DON QUIXOTE MAGAZINE, 536 Columbia,
Lexington, Ky. 40508. Payment in contributors
copies.

DROP CITY NEWSLETTER, Rt. 1, Box 125,
Trinidad, Colorado 81082.

THE DRUMMER, Box 661, Devon, Pa. 19333.
Payment in contributors copy.

DRYAD, 1963-1 Rosemary Hills Dr., Silver
Springs, Md. 20910. Payment in contributors
copies.

DUST, Box 123, El Cerrito, Calif. Payment in contributors copies.

EARLHAM REVIEW, Earlham College, Richmond, Indiana 47374. Payment in contributors copies.

EIKON, P. O. Box 54, Ogunquit, Maine 03907. Payment in contributors copies.

ENCORE MAGAZINE, 1121 Major Ave. NW, Albuquerque, New Mexico 87107. Payment in contributors copy.

ENCOUNTER, P. O. Box 96, St. Leo, Fla. 33574. Payment in contributors copies.

EN GARDE, 19159 Helen, Detroit, Michigan 48234. Payment in contributors copies.

ENTRAILS, 283 East Houston St., Apt. 2, New York, N. Y. 10002. Payment in copies and awards.

EPOCH, 251 Goldwin Smith Hall, Cornell Univ., Ithaca, New York. Payment in contributors copies.

ETC, Box 100, Mill Valley, Calif. 94941. Payment in contributors copies.

EVERGREEN REVIEW, 80 University Place, New York, N. Y. 10003. Pays $25.00 per page.

EXPERIMENT, 6565 NE Windemere Rd., Seattle, Wash. 98105. Payment in contributors copies.

EXPERIMENT, 661 Lewiston Dr., Kirkwood, Mo. 63122. Payment in contributors copies.

THE FAT FROG, 1308 4th Ave., San Francisco, Calif. Payment in contributors copies.

THE FIFTH HORSEMAN, 6929 So. Paxton, Chicago, Ill. 60649. Payment in contributors copies.

FINE ARTS, Box 6837, Cleveland, Ohio 44101. Pays minimum of $5.00 a poem.

FINE ARTS DISCOVERY MAGAZINE, Box 7193, Kansas City, Mo. 64113. Cash awards.

FIRST STAGE, 324 Heavilon Hall, Purdue Univ., Lafayette, Ind. 47907. Payment in contributors copies.

FLOATING BEAR, 23 East 10th St., New York, N. Y. Payment in contributors copies.

FLORIDA QUARTERLY, Room 207, Anderson Hall, University of Florida, Gainesville, Florida 32601. Payment in contributors copies.

FOLIO, P. O. Box 31111, Birmingham, Alabama 35222. Payment in contributors copies.

FORUM, University of Houston, Houston, Texas.

Payment in contributors copies.

FOUR QUARTERS, La Salle College, Olney Ave. at 20th St., Philadelphia, Pa. 19141. Payment varies.

FOXFIRE, Nacoochee School, Robin Gap, Ga. 30568. Payment varies.

FRAGMENTS, 54 W. 88th St., New York, N. Y. 10024. Payment in contributors copies.

FREE LANCE, 4610 Terrace Drive, Niagara Falls, N. Y. 14305. Payment in contributors copies.

FREE LANCE MAGAZINE, 6009 Grand Ave., Cleveland, Ohio 44104. Payment in contributors copies.

FROM THE OTHER SIDE OF SILENCE, 400 W. Franklin, Richmond, Virginia. Pays $1.00 a page plus copies.

FRONTIER PRESS, Box 37, Kensington Sta., Buffalo, New York 14215. Payment in contributors copies.

GALLERY SERIES TWO, 5649 South Harper, Chicago, Ill. 60637. Payment in contributors copies.

GALLEY SAIL REVIEW, P. O. Box 4842, San Francisco, Calif. 94101. Payment in contributors copies.

GATO, P. O. Box 654, Los Gatos, Calif. 95030.
Payment in contributors copies.

GENERATION, 420 Maynard, Ann Arbor, Mich.
Payment in contributors copies.

GEORGIA REVIEW, University of Georgia,
Athens, Georgia 30601. Pays 50¢ a line.

GHOST DANCE, Department of American
Thought & Language, Michigan State University,
East Lansing, Mich. 48823. Payment in con-
tributors copies.

GNOSIS, 372 Pacific St., Brooklyn, N. Y. 11217.
Payment in contributors copies.

GOLDEN ATOM, P. O. Box 1101, Rochester,
N. Y. 14603.

GOLIARDS, P. O. Box 703, San Francisco, Ca.
94101. Payment in contributors copies.

THE GOODLY CO., Comm. Div. Glassboro
State College, Glassboro, New Jersey. Payment
in contributors copies.

GRANDE RONDE REVIEW, 512 19th St.,
Sacramento, Calif. 95814. Payment in contributors copies.

GRAPHOMANIA, P. O. Box 2282, Santa Ana, Ca.
92707.

GREEN GROAD, P. O. Box 4251, Gage Center Station, Topeka, Kansas 66604. Payment in contributors copies.

GREEN KNIGHT PRESS, 45 Hillcrest Road, Amherst, Mass. Pays $10.00 a poem.

THE GUILD QUARTERLY, 317 6th St., Idaho Falls, Idaho 83401.

HAIKU WEST, 111-15 75th Ave., Forest Hills, N. Y. 11375. Awards.

HANGING LOOSE, Box 398, Cooper Sta., New York, N. Y. 10002. Payment in contributors copies.

HARIAN PRESS, P. O. Box 474A, Proctorville, Ohio 45669. Payment in contributors copies.

HARVARD ADVOCATE, 21 South St., Cambridge, Mass. 02138.

HEADS UP, 203 Haddon Hills Apts., Haddonfield, N. J. 08033. Payment in contributors copy.

HIKA, Kenyon College, Gambier, Ohio 43022. Payment in contributors copies.

HIRAM POETRY REVIEW, P. O. Box 162, Hiram, Ohio 44234. Payment in contributors copies.

THE HOBBY HORSE, Joni Roswell, P. O. Box

12431, Charlotte, N. C. 28205.

HOOSIER CHALLENGER MAGAZINE, 8365 Wicklow Ave., Cincinnati, Ohio 45236. Prizes and awards.

THE HUDSON REVIEW, 65 E. 55th St., New York, N. Y. 10022. Pays 50¢ a line.

IDEA AND IMAGE, 15 E. 40th St., New York, N. Y. 10016. Payment varies.

IDLER MAGAZINE, 413 6th St. NE, Washington, D. C. 20002. Payment in contributors copies.

I-KON, 78 East 4th St., New York, N. Y. 10003. Payment in contributors copies.

ILLUMINATIONS, 20 E. King St., Tucson, Ariz. 85705. Payment in contributors copy.

ILLUSTRATED PAPER, P. O. Box 707, Mendocino, Calif. 95460. Payment in contributors copies.

INKY TRAILS, Rt. 2, Box 41-A, Nampa, Idaho 83651. Contest and gift awards.

INNER SPACE, Box 212, Old Chelsea Station, N. Y., N. Y. 10011. Payment in contributors copies.

THE INNER WELL, P. O. Box 274, Marion, Ind. 46752. Pays 10¢ a line.

INTERIM BOOKS, Box 35, New York, N. Y. 10014. Payment in contributors copies.

THE INTERNATIONAL JOURNAL, P. O. Box 175, Irvington, N. J. 07111. Payment in contributors copies.

INTERNATIONAL LANGUAGE REVIEW, P. O. Box 393, Denver, Colorado 80201.

INTREPID, 297 Oakmont Ave., Buffalo, N. Y. 14215. Payment in contributors copies.

IOTA, Idaho State University, Pocatello, Idaho 83201. Payment in contributors copies.

IRENE'S GLOBE-TROTTER, Box 431, DeQuincy, La. 70633.

IT, University Village Apt. 8, Platteville, Wisc. 53818. Payment in contributors copies.

JOHNSONIAN NEWS LETTER, 610 Philosophy Hall, Columbia University, New York, N. Y. 10027.

JOURNAL OF BLACK POETRY, 1308 Masonic Ave. # 4, San Francisco, Calif. 94117. Payment in contributors copies.

JOURNEYBOOK, P. O. Box 4046, Portland, Ore. 97208. Payment in contributors copies.

"JUST THINKING" MAGAZINE, 2038 Jarboe St.,

Kansas City, Mo. 64108. Pays 1¢ a word.

KALEIDOSCOPE, P. O. Box 5457, Milwaukee, Wisc. 53211. Payment in contributors copies.

KANSAS QUARTERLY, Denison Hall, Kansas State University, Manhattan, Kansas 66502. Payment in contributors copies.

KAYAK, 2808 Laguna St., San Francisco, Calif. 94123. Pays $5.00 a page.

KENYON REVIEW, Box 73, Gambier, Ohio 43022. Pays $10.00 a page, first time front of book; $17.00 thereafter.

THE LACE REVIEW, P. O. Box 7181, Roseville Sta., Newark, N. J. 07107. Payment in contributors copies.

THE LADDER, 1005 Market St., Room 208, San Francisco, Calif. 94103.

THE LAMPETER MUSE, Box 662, Bard College, Annandale-on-Hudson, N. Y. 12504. Payment in contributors copies.

LATITUDES, 6102 Sherwood, Houston, Texas 77021. Payment in contributors copies.

LAUREL REVIEW, West Virginia Wesleyan College, Buckhannon, West Va. Payment in contributors copies.

THE LEPRECHAUN REVIEW, 420 East 89th St., New York, N. Y. 10028.

THE LIT, 245 Stanford, Notre Dame, Indiana 46556. Pays $1.00 a poem, plus contributors copy.

LITERARY MAGAZINE OF TUFTS UNIVERSITY, Curtis Hall, Medford, Mass. 02155. Annual contests.

THE LITERARY REVIEW, Fairleigh Dickinson University, Teaneck, N. J. 07666. Payment in contributors copies.

LITERARY TIMES, 2561 N. Clark St., Rooms 228-226, Chicago, Illinois. Pays $2.00 and up for each poem.

LITMUS, Box 385, Berkeley, Calif. 94701. Payment in contributors copies.

THE LITTLE MAGAZINE, 406-74th St., Niagara Falls, New York 14304. Payment in contributors copies.

THE LITTLE SQUARE REVIEW, Flagstaff Rd., Boulder, Colorado 80303.

LIVE OAK, 2140 S. Lone Pine Ave., Springfield, Mo. 65804. Payment in contributors copies.

LONE INDIAN, 1010 Huron Ave., Sheboygan, Wisc. 53081.

LOVELETTER, 2014 Virginia St., Berkeley, Ca. 94709. Payment in contributors copies.

LYRISMOS, 15 Cinderella Ln., East Setauket, N. Y. 11733. Payment in contributors copies.

MACABRE, 91 Westerleigh Rd., New Haven, Conn. 06515. Payment in contributors copies.

MAELSTROM, 310 East 12th St., New York, N. Y. 10003. Payment in contributors copies.

MAELSTROM, Box 688, Blacksburg, Va. 24040.

MAGAZINE, Box 35, New York, N. Y. 10014.

MAGUEY, P. O. Box 385, El Cerrito, Calif. 94530. Payment in contributors copies.

MANDALA, 818 Terry Place, Madison, Wisc. 53711. Payment in contributors copies.

MARK TWAIN JOURNAL, Kirkwood 22, Mo. Payment varies.

MARYS SCRAPBOOK OF POETRY, 7 Sycamore Dr. West, New Hartford, N. Y. 13413.

THE MASSACHUSETTS REVIEW, Memorial Hall, University of Massachusetts, Amherst, Mass. Pays 35¢ per line.

MAY W. WHITNEY, 3908 Rockwell, Spokane, Washington 99205.

MENDOCINO ROBIN, Panpipes Press, 126 Clara Ave., Ukiah, Calif. Payment in contributors copies.

MERLIN'S MAGIC, 318-81st St., Brooklyn, New York 11209. Payment in contributors copies.

METANOIA, 2108 4th Ave. So., Minneapolis, Minn. 55404. Payment in contributors copies.

MICHIGAN QUARTERLY REVIEW, 4010 Administration Bldg., University of Michigan, Ann Arbor, Michigan 48104. Pays 50¢ to $1.00 per line.

THE MIDDLE R, Eastern Oregon College, La Grande, Oregon 97850. Payment in contributors copies.

MIDSTREAM, 515 Park Ave., New York, N. Y. 10022. Pays 50¢ to 75¢ per line.

MIDWEST QUARTERLY, Kansas State College of Pittsburg, Pittsburg, Kansas 66762. Payment in contributors copies.

MIDWESTERN UNIVERSITY QUARTERLY, 3400 Taft, Wichita Falls, Texas 76308. Payment in contributors copies.

MILE HIGH UNDERGROUND, Box 18029 Capitol Hill Sta., Denver, Colorado 80218. Payment in contributors copies.

MINNESOTA REVIEW, Box 4066, Highland Sta.,
St. Paul, Minn. 55116. Pays $15.00 a poem.

MISCELLANEOUS MAN, 938 North Fairfax, Los
Angeles, Calif. 90046. Payment in contributors
copies.

MONOCLE, 80 5th Ave., New York, New York
10011. Pays 3¢ a word.

THE MONTHLY, 2354 S. Race St., Denver,
Colorado 80210.

MONUMENT, & McBaine, Columbia, Mo. 65201.
Payment in contributors copies.

MT. ADAMS REVIEW, P. O. Box 6054, Cincinnati, Ohio 45206. Payment in contributors
copies.

MUNDUS ARTIUM, English Department, Ohio
University, Athens, Ohio 45701. Payment varies.

MUSK, 3100 Benvenue, #3, Berkeley, Calif.
94705. Payment in contributors copies.

MUSTANG REVIEW, 212 South Broadway, Denver, Colorado 80209. Payment in contributors
copies.

NEO MAGAZINE, 1112 Park Ave., New York,
N. Y. 10028. Payment varies.

NEW AMERICAN REVIEW, 1301 Ave. of

Americas, New York, N. Y. 10019. Payment
varies.

NEW CAMPUS REVIEW, 250 West 14th St.,
Denver, Colorado 80204. Payment in contributors
copies.

NEW MEXICO QUARTERLY, University of New
Mexico Press, Albuq., New Mexico 87106.

NEW SOUTH QUARTERLY, 740 France St.,
Baton Rouge, La. 70806. Payment in contributors
copies.

NEW STUDENT REVIEW, Box 40, Norton Union
St., University of New York, Buffalo, New York.

THE NINTH CIRCLE, 1201 University Ave.,
Las Cruces, New Mexico 88001. Payment in
contributors copies.

NORTH AMERICAN MENTOR, John Westburg,
Conesville, Iowa 52739. Awards.

NORTHEAST, 1310 Shorewood Dr., La Crosse,
Wisc. 54601. Payment in contributors copies.

A NOSEGAY IN BLACK, 20 Benton Place,
St. Louis, Mo. 63104. Payment in contributors
copies.

OCCIDENT, Eshleman Hall, University of Calif.,
Berkeley, Calif. 94720. Payment in contributors
copies.

OPEN PLACES, 107 Westwood Ave., Columbia, Mo. 65201. Payment in contributors copies.

ONE TWO ONE, 58-15 263 St., Little Neck, N. Y. 11362. Payment in contributors copies.

OPINION, P. O. Box 9019, Chicago, Ill. 60690.

ORIGINAL WORKS, Department of French and Italian, University of S. Calif., Los Angeles, Ca. 90007. Payment in contributors copies.

ORION MAGAZINE, CSA Press, Lakemont, Ga. 30552. Payment in contributors copies.

THE OTHER, 839 N. Marshall St., Milwaukee, Wisc. 53202. Payment in contributors copies.

OUTCAST, P. O. Box 2182, Santa Fe, New Mex. 87501. Pays poets out of the profits. $2.00 min.

OUTLET, P. O. Box 662, Manhattan, Kansas 66502. Payment in contributors copies.

THE OUTSIDER, 1009 East Elm, Tucson, Ariz.

OUT THERE MAGAZINE, 467 1/2 N. Orange Grove Ave., Los Angeles, Calif. 90036. Payment in contributors copies.

OX HEAD PRESS, 1210 15th Ave., Menomonie, Wisc. 54751. Payment 25 copies plus royalty.

PAINTED POETRY APPRECIATION, 710 Montgomery Rd. , Tuskegee Institute, Alabama 36088.

PAN AMERICAN REVIEW, 1100 W. Samano, Edinburg, Texas 78539. Payment in contributors copies.

PAPER TIGER, 245 Rutland St. , Roxbury, Mass. 02119.

PAPERBAG MAGAZINE, 3100 Riverside Dr. , Los Angeles, Calif. 90027. Payment varies.

THE PARIS REVIEW, 45-39 171 Place, Flushing, New York 11358. Pays 35¢ a line.

PARTISAN REVIEW, 542 George St. , New Brunswick, N. J. 08903. Pays 1 1/2¢ a word.

PATHWAYS, P. O. Box 2000, Vacaville, Calif. 95688. Payment in contributors copies.

PENMAN, 133 W. 6th St. , Deer Park, New York 11729. Pays 10¢ to $3. 00.

PENUMBRA, 8-20 Fair Lawn Ave. , Fair Lawn, New Jersey. Payment in contributors copies.

PER SE, Box 2377, Stanford, Calif. 94305. Payment in contributors copies.

THE PERSONALIST, University of Southern California, Los Angeles, Calif. 90007.

PERSPECTIVE, Washington Univ. , St. Louis,

Mo. 61630. Payment in contributors copies.

PH !, 217 East 12th St., 1R, New York, N. Y. 10003.

PHOENIX, Phoenix Publications, 619 West Main, Independence, Kansas 67301. Payment varies.

THE PHOENIX, Phoenix House, 1333 E. Linwood Blvd., Kansas City, Mo. 64109.

PIERIAN SPRING, Box 1009, Ft. Collins, Colo. 80521. Payment in contributors copies.

PIXIE ANGEL, 8635 Elm St., Los Angeles, Calif. 90002. Pays 1¢ a poem with a certificate.

PLUME & SWORD, Box 85, Newcomb Hall Sta., University of Virginia, Charlottesville, Virginia. Payment in contributors copies.

PN2 EXPERIMENT, 1606 Sanderson Ave., Scranton, Pa. 18509. Payment in contributors copies.

POETIC LICENSE, P. O. Box 12141, St. Petersburg, Fla. 33733. Payment in contributors copies.

POETRY CLUB MAGAZINE, Rt. 2, Windsor, Mo. 65360.

POETRY NORTHWEST, Parrington Hall, Univ. of Washington, Seattle, Wash. 98105. Payment in contributors copies.

POETRY PREVUE, 88 Church Ave., Brooklyn, New York 11218.

POETRY REVIEW, University of Tampa, Tampa, Forida 33606. Payment in contributors copies.

POETRY VENTURE, 8245 26th Ave. N., St. Petersburg, Fla. 33710. Payment in contributors copies.

PORTLAND REVIEW, University of Portland, Portland, Oregon 97203. Payment in contributors copies.

PRAIRIE SCHOONER, Andrews Hall, University of Nebraska, Lincoln, Nebraska 68508. Payment in contributors copies.

PREMIERE, 32 Waverly St., Belmont, Mass. 02178. Payment in contributors copies.

PROJECT, 1172 W. Hancock, Detroit, Mich. 48201. Payment in contributors copies.

PYRAMID, 32 Waverly St., Belmont, Mass. 02178. Payment in contributors copies.

QUARTERLY, Montclair State College, Upper Montclair, N. J. 07043.

QUARTERLY REVIEW OF LITERATURE, Box 287, Bard College, Annandale-on-Hudson, N. Y.

12504. Payment varies.

QUARTET, 246 Sylvia St., W. Lafayette, Ind. 47906. Pays $1.00 a poem, plus contributors copies.

THE QUEST, P. O. Box 207, Cathedral Sta., New York, N. Y. 10025. Payment in contributors copies.

QUIXOTE, 315 North Brooks, Madison, Wisc. 53703. Payment in contributors copies.

RADICAL AMERICA, 1237 Spaight St., Madison, Wisc. 53703.

THE RAG, 609 West 23rd, Austin, Texas 78705.

RAINBOW, Phoenix Publications, 2191 Harbor Blvd., Sp. A-3, Costa Mesa, Calif. 92627.

READERS & WRITERS, 130-21 224th St., Jamaica, New York 11413.

REALITY, P. O. Box 271, New Vernon, N. J. 07976. Payment in contributors copies.

RED CEDAR REVIEW, 325 Morrill Hall, Michigan State University, East Lansing, Mich. 48823. Payment in contributors copies.

RED CLAY READER, Sharon Hills, Charlotte, N. C. 28210. Pays $7.00 to $25.00 a poem.

ROANOKE REVIEW, Roanoke College, Salem, Virginia 24153.

ROUNDTABLE, 96 Falmouth St., Portland, Me. 04103. Payment in contributors copies.

RUNCIBLE SPOON, P. O. Box 4622, Sacramento, Calif. 95825. Payment in contributors copies.

SALMAGUNDI, P. O. Box 768, Flushing, N. Y. 11355. Pays $5.00 a poem.

THE SALT CREEK READER, 2820 R. St., Lincoln, Nebraska 68503. Payment in contributors copies.

SAND SCRIPT, P. O. Box 313, San Bruno, Ca. 94066. Payment in contributors copies.

THE SAN FRANCISCO EARTHQUAKE, 1562 Grant Ave., San Francisco, Calif. 94133. Payment in contributors copies.

S-B GAZETTE, P. O. Box 731, Sausalito, Ca. 94965. Payment in contributors copies.

SCOPECRAEFT, Department of English, N. D. S. U., Fargo, North Dakota 58102. Payment in contributors copies.

SEWANEE REVIEW, University of the South, Sewanee, Tenn. Pays 50¢ a line.

THE SHAKESPEARE NEWSLETTER, University

of Illinois at Chicago Circle, Chicago, Ill. 60680.
Payment in contributors copies.

SHENANDOAH, The Washington and Lee University Review, Box 772, Lexington, Va. 24450.
Payment varies.

SILO, Bennington College, Bennington, Vermont
05201. Payment in contributors copies.

SIMBOLICA, 63 Mercury Ave., Tibouron, Calif.
94920. Payment in contributors copies.

SMALL COMFORT, 18 N. Mentor, Pasadena,
Calif. Payment varies.

THE SMALL POND, 39 Josslyn St., Auburn,
Maine 04210. Payment in contributors copies.

THE SMITH, 5 Beekman St., New York, N. Y.
10038. Pays $2.00 to $6.00 a poem.

SNOWY EGRET, 416 Franklin, Cambridge,
Mass. 02139. Pays $2.00 a poem.

SOLILOQUY, 201 Morrill Hall, Oklahoma State
University, Stillwater, Okla. 74074.

SOUTH DAKOTA REVIEW, Box 111, University
Exchange, Vermillion, S. D. 57069. Payment
in contributors copies.

SOUTH FLORIDA POETRY JOURNAL, FAH
265, University of South Florida, Tampa, Fla.

33620.   Payment in contributors copies.

SOUTH FLORIDA REVIEW, 223 University
Center, University of South Florida, Tampa, Fla.
33620.   Payment in contributors copies.

SOUTHERN HUMANITITES REVIEW, 212 Sam-
ford Hall, Auburn University, Auburn, Alabama
36380.   Payment in contributors copies.

THE SOUTHERN REVIEW, Drawer D, Univ.
Sta., Baton Rouge, La. 70803.   Pays $20 a page.

SOUTHWEST REVIEW, Southern Methodist Univ.
Dallas, Texas 75222.   Pays $5 a poem.

THE SPARROW, 103 Waldron St., West Lafayette, Ind. 47906.   Payment in contributors copies.

SPECTRUM, Noel Young Press, Box 11762,
Goleta, Calif. 93101.   Pays 50¢ a line.

SPERO, 1850 N. Orchard, Chicago, Ill. 60614.
Payment in contributors copies.

STEPPENWOLF, P. O. Box 55045, Omaha, Neb.
68155.   Payment in contributors copies.

STONE, 26 Dublin Rd., Pennington, New Jersey
08534.   Payment in copies.

SUNRISE-SUNSET-SILHOUETTE, Potvin Street,
Claremont, N. H. 03743.

SUNSHINE MAGAZINE, The House of Sunshine, Litchfield, Ill.

TANGENTS, 3473 1/2 Cahuenga Blvd., Hollywood Calif. 90028. Payment in contributors copies.

TERRY'S HOBBY CLUB, Kearns, Utah 84118.

TEXAS CLARION, 509 Virginia St., Wichita Falls, Texas 76301.

THE TEXAS QUARTERLY, Box 7517, Univ. Station, Austin, Texas 78712. Pays 80¢ a line.

THE THINKER, Jan Shupp, 325 E. 11 St., Lebanon, Pa. 17042.

THIS AND ... , 807 Furnald, Columbia Univ., New York, N. Y. 10027. Payment in contributors copies.

THOUGHT, Fordham University, 441 E. Fordham Rd., Bronx, New York 10458.

TIME & TIDE, P. O. Box 25, Lorton, Virginia 22079. Payment in contributors copies.

TOCSIN, 1047 23rd St., Des Moines, Iowa 50311. Payment in contributors copies.

TOLAR CREEK SYNDICATE, Box 4875, Univ. Park, New Mexico 88001. Payment in contributors copies.

TRACE, P. O. Box 1068, Hollywood, California. Payment varies.

TRI-QUARTERLY, University Hall 101, Northwestern University, Evanston, Illinois. Pays $1 a line.

TRUMPET, 6400 Forest Lane, Dallas, Texas 75230. Payment in contributors copies.

TULSA POETRY QUARTERLY, 204 East 45th Place, Tulsa, Okla. 74105. Payment in contributors copies, plus prizes.

TWIGS, Box 7, Pikeville College, Pikeville, Ky. 41501.

UBRIS, 106B Lord Hall, University of Maine, Orono, Maine 04473.

THE UNDERGROUND RAILROAD, 129 Lock St., Lockport, New York 14094. Payment in contributors copies.

UNICORN FOLIO, Studios 126 & 127, El Paseo, Santa Barbara, Calif. 93101. Payment in contributors copies.

THE VIRGINIA QUARTERLY REVIEW, 1 West Range, Charlottesville, Va. Pays 50¢ a line.

VECTOR, 83 Sixth St., San Francisco, Calif. 94102. Payment in contributors copies.

VOICES INTERNATIONAL, Box 325, Piggott, Arkansas 72454. Payment in contributors copy.

VOYAGES, Box 4862, Washington, D. C. 20008. Pays 35¢ to 50¢ a line.

WESTERN HUMANITIES REVIEW, University of Utah, Salt Lake City, Utah 84112. Payment in contributors copies.

WESTERN REVIEW, Western New Mexico Univ., Silver City, New Mexico.

W-HOLLOW HARVEST, Box 46-154, Cincinnati, Ohio 45246. Payment in contributors copies.

THE WILLIE, 1379 Masonic, San Francisco, Calif. 94117. Payment in contributors copies.

WIN PEACE & FREEDOM THROUGH NON-VIOLENT ACTION, 5 Beekman St., New York, N. Y. 10038.

WISCONSIN REVIEW, Wisconsin State University Oshkosh, Wisc. 54901. Payment in contributors copies and sometimes $1 per column of print.

WORDJOCK, 730 Mill St., Tipton, Indiana 46072. Payment in contributors copies.

WORKS, AMS Press, 56 E. 13th St., New York, N. Y. 10003. Pays 50¢ a line.

WORMWOOD REVIEW, Box 111, Storrs, Conn.

06268. Payment in contributors copies.

WRITER'S FORUM, 288 Piermont Ave., South Nyack, New York 10960. Payment in contributors copies.

WRITER'S NOTES & QUOTES, 142 W. Brookdale, Fullerton, Calif. 92632. Payment in contributors copies and awards.

WRITINGS, 5 Beekman St., New York, N. Y. 10038. Payment in contributors copies and cash awards.

ZEITGEIST, Box 150, East Lansing, Michigan 48823. Payment in contributors copies and cash awards.

ZENARCHY, 2803 Marlin, Tampa, Florida 33611. Payment in contributors copies.

0 TO 9, Vito Hannibal Acconci, 383 Broome St., New York, N. Y. 10013. Payment in contributors copies.

*REGIONAL AND TRAVEL MAGAZINES

APPALACHIAN REVIEW, 307 Armstrong Hall, West Virginia University, Morgantown, W. Va. 26506. Pays 50¢ a line.

ARIZONA HIGHWAY, 2039 W. Lewis, Phoenix, Ariz. 85009.

ASIA CALLING, 881 Via de la Paz, Pacific Palisades, Calif. 90272.

BOSTON MAGAZINE, 125 High St., Boston, Mass. 02110.

THE CALLER, P. O. Box 647, Waco, Texas 76703. Pays $2.50 a poem.

CARIBBEAN BEACHCOMBER, 210 Ponce de Leon Ave., San Juan, Puerto Rico 00901. Pays $2.00 to $5.00 a poem.

CHICAGOLAND, 333 North Michigan Ave., Chicago, Ill. Pays $5.00 and up for each poem.

THE DULUTHIAN, 220 Medical Arts Building, Duluth, Minn. 55802. Payment varies.

FOCUS MIDWEST, P. O. Box 3086, St. Louis, Mo. 63130. Payment varies.

NEW ENGLAND GALAXY, Old Sturbridge Village, Sturbridge, Mass. Pays $50.00 a poem.

NEW HAMPSHIRE PROFILES, 1 Pleasant St., Portsmouth, N. H. Pays $2.00 to $5.00 a poem.

OHIO MOTORIST, 2605 Euclid Ave., Cleveland, Ohio 44115. Pays $5.00 to $10.00 a poem.

OHIO RIVER MAGAZINE, P. O. Box 2023, Cincinnati, Ohio 45201.

PROMENADE MAGAZINE, 40 E. 49th St., New York, N. Y. 10017. Pays $1.00 to $1.50 a line.

TEXAS METRO MAGAZINE, P. O. Drawer 1166, Arlington, Texas 76010. Payment varies.

WESTWAYS, 2601 S. Figuerea St., Los Angeles, Calif. 90054. Pays 50¢ a line.

YANKEE, INC., Main St., Dublin, N. H. 03444. Payment varies.

*RELIGIOUS MAGAZINES

ADULT BIBLE STUDY BOOK, 1816 Chestnut St., Philadelphia, Pa. 19103. Payment varies.

ALL-CHURCH PRESS, INC., P. O. Box 1159, Fort Worth, Tex. 76109. Payment varies.

ANNIE'S ALMANAC, 453 Maple Ave., New Martinville, West Virginia 26155. Payment varies.

BAPTIST HERALD, 7308 Madison St., Forest Park, Illinois 60131. Payment varies.

BAPTIST LEADER, Valley Forge, Penn. Pays 25¢ a line.

BETHANY GUIDE, Box 179, St. Louis, Mo. 63166. Pays 25¢ a line.

BIBLE SCHOOL JOURNAL, 6401 The Pasco, Kansas City, Mo. 64131. Payment varies.

CAMPUS AMBASSADOR MAGAZINE, 1445 Boonville Ave., Springfield, Mo. 65802. Pays 1/2 ¢ a word.

CATHOLIC RURAL LIFE, 3801 Grand Ave., Des Moines, Iowa. Payment varies.

THE CHICAGO JEWISH FORUM, 173 W. Madison St., Chicago, Illinois 60602. Pays $15.00 a page.

THE CHRISTIAN, Box 179, St. Louis, Missouri 63166. Pays $1.00 to $5.00 a poem.

THE CHRISTIAN CENTURY, 407 S. Dearborn St., Chicago, Ill. 60605.

CHRISTIAN HERALD, 27 E. 39th St., New York, N.Y. 10016. Pays $5.00 to $10.00 a poem.

THE CHRISTIAN HOME, 201 Eighth Ave. South, Nashville, Tenn. 37203. Pays 50¢ a line.

CHRISTIANITY TODAY, 1014 Washington Bldg., Washington, D.C. 20005. Pays $10.00 a poem.

CHURCH ADMINISTRATION, 127 Ninth Ave. N., Nashville, Tenn. 37203. Pays 35¢ a line.

THE CHURCH MUSICIAN, 127 Ninth Ave. N., Nashville, Tenn. 37203. Pays $5.00 to $10.00

a poem.

COLUMBIA, P. O. Drawer 1670, New Haven, Conn. 06507. Pays $25.00 a poem.

THE CONGREGATIONALIST, 176 W. Wisconsin Ave., Milwaukee, Wisc. 53203. Payment varies.

CONQUEST, 6410 The Pasco, Kansas City, Mo. 64131. Pays 10¢ a line.

DAILY MEDITATION, P. O. Box 2710, San Antonio, Texas 78206. Pays 14¢ a line.

DAILY WORD, Lee's, Summit, Mo. Pays 25¢ and up a line.

DECISION MAGAZINE, 1300 Harmon Place, Minneapolis, Minn. 55403. Payment varies.

THE EPISCOPALIAN, 1930 Chestnut St., Philadelphia, Pa. 19103. Payment varies.

ETERNITY MAGAZINE, 1716 Spruce St., Philadelphia, Pa. 19103. Pays $10.00 to $15.00 per poem.

FRANCISCAN MESSAGE, Franciscan Publishers, Pulaski, Wisconsin. Pays $2.00 to $10.00 per poem.

GOOD NEWS, 422 South 5th St., Minneapolis, Minn. 55415. Payment varies.

GOSPEL HERALD, Scottsdale, Penn.

GREATER WORKS, 422 S. Fifth St. , Minneapolis, Minn. 55415. Pays $5.00 to $50.00 a poem.

HEARTHSTONE, MPO Box 179, St. Louis, Mo. 63166.

HIS, 130 N. Wells St. , Chicago, Ill. 60606. Pays $5.00 to $10.00 a poem.

HOME LIFE, 127 Ninth Ave. North, Nashville, Tenn. 37203. Payment varies. $2.50 min.

INTERACTION, 3558 S. Jefferson, St. Louis, Mo. 63118. Pays $5.00 to $15.00 a poem.

LIBERTY, 6840 Eastern Ave. N. W. , Washington, D. C. 20012. Pays $5.00 to $10.00 a poem.

LIGHT AND LIFE EVANGEL, Winona Lake, Ind. 46590. Pays 20¢ a line.

LIGHTED PATHWAY, 922 Montgomery Ave. , Cleveland, Tenn. 37311. Payment varies.

THE LITTLE FLOWER MAGAZINE, 7907 Bellaire Blvd. , Houston, Texas 77036. Payment varies.

THE LIVING CHURCH, 407 E. Michigan St. , Milwaukee, Wisc. 53202.

THE LUTHERAN STANDARD, 426 South 5th St. ,

Minneapolis, Minnesota 55415. Pays $5.00 per poem.

LUTHERAN TEACHER, Augsburg Publishing House, 426 South Fifth St., Minneapolis, Minn. 55415.

THE MAGNIFICAT, 131 Laurel St., Box 154, Manchester, N. H.

MARRIAGE, St. Meinrad, Ind. 47577. Payment varies.

MESSAGE MAGAZINE, Box 59, Nashville, Tenn. 37202. Pays 25¢ a line.

MESSENGER, 1451 Dundee Ave., Elgin, Illinois 60120. Payment varies.

THE MIRACULOUS MEDAL, 475 E. Chelten Ave., Philadelphia, Pa. 19144. Pays 50¢ and up a line.

OMI MISSION MAGAZINE, Box 96, San Antonio, Tex. 78206. Payment varies.

OUR LADY OF THE SNOWS, Belleville, Ill. 62223. Payment varies.

THE PENTECOSTAL EVANGEL, 1445 Boon-ville, Springfield, Mo. 65802. Pays 20¢ for each line.

PRESBYTERIAN SURVEY, 341 Ponce de Leon

Ave. N. E., Atlanta, Georgia 30308. Pays $2.50
to $5.00 a poem.

QUEEN OF ALL HEARTS, 40 South Saxon Ave.,
Bay Shore, New York 11706. Payment varies.

THE REIGN OF THE SACRED HEART, Hales
Corners, Wisconsin 53130. Pays $5.00 for each
poem.

REVIEW FOR RELIGIOUS, 612 Humboldt Bldg.,
539 North Grand Blvd., St. Louis, Missouri
63103. Payment varies.

SALESIAN STUDIES, 5401 Sargent Rd., Hyatts-
ville, Md. 20782. Payment varies.

SCIENCE OF MIND MAGAZINE, 3251 West 6th
St., Los Angeles, Calif. 90005. Pays $3.00 to
$10.00 a poem.

THE SIGN, Union City, N. J. Pays $10.00 for
each poem.

SIGNS OF THE TIMES, 1350 Villa, Mountain
View, Calif. 94041. Pays $10.00 a poem.

SUNDAY DIGEST, 850 North Grove Ave., Elgin,
Ill. 60120. Pays 4¢ or 5¢ a word.

SUNDAY SCHOOL WORLD, 1816 Chestnut St.,
Philadelphia, Pennsylvania 19103. Payment
varies.

TEACH MAGAZINE, 725 E. Colorado, Glendale, Calif. 91205. Pays 50¢ a line.

THE TEXAS METHODIST, P. O. Box 547, Irving, Tex. 75060. Payment varies.

THIS DAY, 3558 South Jefferson Ave. , St. Louis, Mo. 63118. Pays 50¢ a line.

TOGETHER, Box 423, Park Ridge, Ill. 60068. Pays $10. 00 to $15. 00 a poem.

VISION, P. O. Box 179, St. Louis, Mo. 63166. Payment varies.

THE WAR CRY, 860 North Dearborn Street, Chicago, Illinois 60610. Pays $2. 00 to $5. 00 for each poem.

THE WAY, Mennonite Publishing House, Scottdale, Pa. Pays 10¢ a line.

WEEKLY UNITY, Unity School of Christianity, Lee's Summit, Mo. 64063. Payment varies.

*SCIENCE FICTION MAGAZINES

FANTASY AND SCIENCE FICTION, 347 East 53rd St. , New York, New York 10022. Pays $10 and up for each poem.

OUT THERE MAGAZINE, 467 1/2 N. Orange Grove Ave. , Los Angeles, Calif. 90036.

*SPORT AND OUTDOOR MAGAZINES

THE BACKSTRETCH, 19363 James Couzens Highway, Detroit, Mich. 48235.

CYCLE NEWS, 6477 N. Long Beach Blvd., Long Beach, California 90805. Pays 50¢ for each column inch.

GOLF DIGEST, 88 Scribner Ave., Norwalk, Conn. Pays $5.00 for each poem.

NATIONAL PARKS MAGAZINE, 1701 18th St., N. W., Washington, D. C. 20009. Pays 50¢ per line.

OUTDOOR WORLD, 1600 Tullie Circle N. E., Atlanta, Ga. 30329. Payment varies.

PRIVATE PILOT, 7120 Hayvenhurst Ave., Van Nuys, Calif. 91406. Pays $5.00 to $50.00 for each poem.

THE RUDDER, 67 West 44th St., New York, N. Y. 10036. Payment varies.

SKATING, 178 Tremont St., Boston, Mass. 02111. Payment varies.

THE SKIPPER, Second St. at Spa Creek, Annapolis, Md. 21404. Pays 30¢ a line.

SKIWEEK, 88 Scribner Ave., Norwalk, Conn. 06856. Payment varies.

SURFER, P. O. Box 1028, Dana Point, Calif. Payment varies.

SWIMMING WORLD, 12618 Killion St., North Hollywood, Calif.

WESTERN SKIER, 1933 Union St., San Francisco, Calif. 94123. Payment varies.

*THEATER, MOVIE, TV AND ENTERTAINMENT MAGAZINES

FILM QUARTERLY, University of California Press, Berkeley, California 94720. Payment varies.

THEATRE USA, 6300 W. Greenfield Ave., West Allis, Wisc. 53214.

*WOMEN'S MAGAZINES

BABY TALK, 149 Madison Ave., New York, N. Y. 10016. Pays $5.00 to $10.00 a poem.

COSMOPOLITAN, 1775 Broadway, New York, N. Y. 10019. Payment varies.

EXPECTING, 52 Vanderbilt Ave., New York, N. Y. 10017. Payment varies.

FAMILY CIRCLE MAGAZINE, 488 Madison Ave., New York, N. Y. 10022. Pays $25.00 and up for each poem.

GOOD HOUSEKEEPING, 959 Eighth Ave., New York, N. Y. 10019. Pays $5.00 per line.

HARPER'S BAZAAR, 717 Fifth Ave., New York, N. Y. 10022. Pays $1.00 per line.

MADEMOISELLE, 420 Lexington Ave., New York, N. Y. 10017. Pays $25.00 a poem.

McCALL'S, 230 Park Ave., New York, N. Y. 10017. Pays $5.00 a poem.

MODERN BRIDE, 1 Park Ave., New York, N.Y. 10016. Pays $10.00 to $15.00 a poem.

U. S. LADY, P. O. Box 8156, Washington, D. C. 20024. Pays $2.00 to $10.00 a poem.

VOGUE, 420 Lexington Ave., New York, N. Y. 10017.

YOUR NEW BABY, 52 Vanderbilt Ave., New York, N. Y. 10017. Payment varies.

*COMPANY PUBLICATIONS

THE AIRWAY PIONEER, P. O. Box 530, Santa Rosa, Calif. 95432. Payment varies.

BI B-LINER, Braniff Bldg., Exchange Park, Dallas, Texas 75235.

NUGGETS, 1100 Waterway Blvd., Indianapolis, Ind. 46202. Payment varies.

PEN, 444 Sherman St., Denver, Colorado 80203. Pays 50¢ a line.

STORE CHAT, 801 Market St., Philadelphia, Pa. 19105. Payment varies.

*BOOK TRADE

THE HORN BOOK MAGAZINE, 585 Boylston St., Boston, Mass. 02116. Pays $10.00 to $15.00 a poem.

LIBRARY JOURNAL, 1180 Ave. of the Americas, New York, N. Y. 10036.

*EDUCATION

TODAY'S CATHOLIC TEACHER, 38 West Fifth St., Dayton, Ohio 45402. Pays $5.00 to $20.00 for a poem.

*ELECTRICITY

COUNTRY LIVING MAGAZINE, 4302 Indianola Ave., Columbus, Ohio 43214.

*GROCERIES

DELI NEWS, P. O. Box 706, Hollywood, Calif. 90028. Payment varies.

*HOSPITALS, HEALTH AND NURSING

AMERICAN JOURNAL OF NURSING, 10 Columbus Circle, New York, N. Y. 10019. Payment varies.

*JOURNALISM

AUTHOR/POET, P. O. Box 2127, Birmingham, Ala. 35201. Prizes.

WRITER'S DIGEST, 22 E. 12th St., Cincinnati, Ohio 45210. Pays 50¢ a line.

*MUSIC

MUSIC MINISTRY, 201 Eighth Ave. South, Nashville, Tenn. Pays 50¢ a line.

*PRINTING

PLAN AND PRINT, 33 E. Congress Parkway, Chicago, Ill. 60605. Pays $5.00 a poem.

*RADIO, TELEVISION, ELECTRONICS AND
COMMUNICATIONS

ELECTRONIC TECHNICIAN/DEALER, Ojibway
Press, Ojibway Bldg., Duluth, Minn. 55802. Pays
$5.00 to $7.50 a poem.

*POETRY BOOK PUBLISHERS

ABINGDON PRESS, 201 Eighth Ave. South,
Nashville, Tenn. 37203.

AMERICAN HERITAGE PUBLISHING CO., INC.
551 Fifth Ave., New York, N. Y. 10017

THE AMERICAN HUNGARIAN REVIEW, 5410
Kerth Rd., St. Louis, Mo. 63128.

ARCO PUBLISHING CO, INC., 219 Park Ave.
South, New York, N. Y. 10003.

ARKHAM HOUSE: PUBLISHERS, Sauk City,
Wisc. 53583.

A. S. BARNES & CO., INC., Box 421, Cran-
bury, N. J. 08512.

ASTOR-HONOR, INC., 26 E. 442nd St., New
York, N. Y. 10017.

ATHENEUM PUBLISHERS, 122 E. 42nd St.,
New York, N. Y. 10017.

ATLANTIC MONTHLY PRESS, 8 Arlington St., Boston, Mass. 02116.

AUGSBURG PUBLISHING HOUSE, 426 S. Fifth St., Minneapolis, Minn. 55415.

BEACON PRESS, 25 Beacon St., Boston, Mass. 02108.

BELLA VISTA PRESS, 1110 Valley View Dr., Fayetteville, Ark. 72701.

THE BETHANY PRESS, Beaumont and Pine Blvd., Box 179, St. Louis, Mo. 63166.

BRANDEN PRESS, INC., 36 Melrose St., Boston, Mass. 02116.

CHARLES T. BRANFORD, CO., 28 Union St., Newton Centre 59, Mass.

CENTURY HOUSE, INC., Yorker Yankee Village Museum, Watkins Glen, N. Y. 14891.

CHILTON BOOK CO., 401 Walnut St., Philadelphia, Pa. 19106.

CITADEL PRESS, 222 Park Ave. South, New York, N. Y. 10003.

COWLES EDUCATION COR., 488 Madison Ave., N. Y., N. Y. 10022.

COYOTE BOOKS, 1562 Grant Ave., San Francisco, Calif. 94133.

CRESCENDO PUBLISHERS, 48-50 Melrose St.,
Boston, Mass. 02116.

THOMAS Y. CROWELL CO., 201 Park Ave.,
South, New York, N. Y. 10003.

DA CAPO PRESS, 227 W. 17th St., New York,
N. Y. 10011.

DELL PUBLISHING CO., INC., 750 Third Ave.
N. Y., N. Y.

DODD, MEAD AND CO., 79 Madison Ave.,
New York, N. Y. 10016.

DOR-NIC PUBLISHERS, Bruceville, Ind. 47516.

E. P. DUTTON & CO., INC., 201 Park Ave.,
South, N. Y., N. Y. 10003.

EVERETT/EDWARDS, INC., 133 South Pecan
Ave., DeLand, Fla. 32720.

FEDERAL LEGAL PUBLICATIONS, INC., 96
Morton St., N. Y., N. Y. 10014.

FLEET PRESS COR., 156 Fifth Ave., New
York, N. Y. 10010.

THE C. R. GIBSON CO., Knight St., Norwalk,
Conn. 06852.

GROSSET & DUNLAP, INC., 51 Madison Ave., N. Y., N. Y. 10010.

HARCOURT, BRACE & WORLD, INC., 757 Third Ave. at 47th St., N. Y., N. Y. 10017.

HARVARD UNIVERSITY PRESS, 79 Garden St., Cambridge, Mass. 02138.

HASTINGS HOUSE PUBLISHERS, INC., 10 E. 40th St., N. Y., N. Y. 10016.

HERALD HOUSE, P. O. Box 1019, Independence, Mo. 64051.

HERMAN PUBLISHING SERVICE, INC., 25 Huntington Ave., Boston, Mass. 02116.

HOLT, RINEHART AND WINSTON, INC., 383 Madison Ave., N. Y., N. Y. 10017.

HORS COMMERCE PRESS, 22526 Shadycroft Ln., Torrance, Calif.

HOUGHTON MIFFLIN CO., 2 Park St., Boston 7, Mass.

BRUCE HUMPHRIES PUBLISHERS, 68 Beacon St., Somerville, Mass. 02143.

THE JOHNS HOPKINS PRESS, Baltimore, Md. 21218.

LIVING BOOKS, LTD., 11 West 42nd St., New

York, N. Y. 10036.

ROBERT B. LUCE, INC., 1244 19th St., N. W., Washington, D. C. 20036.

MANYLAND BOOKS, INC., Box 266 Wall St. Station, N. Y., N. Y. 10005.

McGRAW-HILL BOOK CO., 330 West 42nd St., N. Y., N. Y. 10036.

DAVID McKAY CO., INC., 750 Third Ave., N. Y., N. Y. 10017.

MICHIGAN STATE UNIVERSITY PRESS, Box 550, East Lansing, Mich. 48823.

WILLIAM MORROW & CO., 425 Park Ave. S., New York, N. Y. 10016.

THE NAYLOR CO., 1015 Culebra, P. O. Box 1838, San Antonio, Texas 78206.

NEW YORK UNIVERSITY PRESS, 62 Fifth Ave. N. Y., N. Y. 10011.

W. W. NORTON & CO., INC., 55 Fifth Ave., N. Y., N. Y. 10003.

OCTOBER HOUSE, INC., 55 W. 13th St., New York, N. Y. 10011.

OHIO STATE UNIVERSITY PRESS, 2070 Neil Ave., Columbus, Ohio 43210.

OHIO UNIVERSITY PRESS, Athens, Ohio.

THE PEMBERTON PRESS, 1 Pemberton Parkway, Austin, Texas 78703.

THE PEQUOT PRESS, INC., Stonington, Conn. 06378.

PHILOSOPHICAL LIBRARY, PUBLISHERS, 15 E. 40th St., N. Y., N. Y. 10016.

PTERODACTYL PRESS, 1451 McAllister St., San Francisco, Calif. 94115.

BERN PORTER BOOKS, 4 Church St., Belfast, Maine 04915.

RANDOM HOUSE, INC., 457 Madison Ave., New York, N. Y. 10022.

RED DUST, INC., 229 East 81st St., New York, N. Y. 10028.

REILLY & LEE CO., 114 W. Illinois St., Chicago, Ill. 60610.

RUTGERS UNIVERSITY PRESS, 30 College Ave. New Brunswick, N. J. 08903.

CHARLES SCRIBNER'S SONS, 597 Fifth Ave., N. Y., N. Y. 10017.

SIMON & SCHUSTER TRADE BOOK DIVISION, 630 Fifth Ave., N. Y., N. Y. 10020.

RICHARD R. SMITH CO., Noone House, Peterborough, N. H.

SMYRNA PRESS, Box 418, Stuyvesant Station, N. Y., N. Y. 10009.

STATE UNIVERSITY OF NEW YORK PRESS, Thurlow Terrace, Albany, N. Y. 12201.

THE THOMIST PRESS, 487 Michigan Ave., N. E., Washington, D. C. 20017.

UNITED CHURCH PRESS, 1505 Race St., Philadelphia, Pa. 19102.

UNIVERSITY OF MASSACHUSETTS PRESS, Munson Hall, Amherst, Mass. 01002.

UNIVERSITY OF MISSOURI PRESS, Columbia, Missouri.

UNIVERSITY OF NEBRASKA PRESS, 901 N. 17th St., Lincoln, Nebr. 68508.

UNIVERSITY OF NORTH CAROLINA PRESS, Box 510, Chapel Hill, N. C.

UNIVERSITY OF TEXAS PRESS, University Station, Austin, Texas 78712.

UNIVERSITY OF UTAH PRESS, University of Utah, Salt Lake City, Utah 84112.

THE UNIVERSITY PRESS OF VIRGINIA, Box

3608, University Sta., Charlottesville, Virginia.

UNIVERSITY PRESS OF KANSAS, 358 Watson Library, Lawrence, Kansas 66044.

WASHINGTON SQUARE PRESS, INC., 630 Fifth Ave., N. Y., N. Y. 10020.

WAYNE STATE UNIVERSITY PRESS, Detroit, Mich. 48202.

WESLEYAN UNIVERSITY PRESS, Wesleyan Station, Middletown, Conn. 06457.

WHITMORE PUBLISHING CO., 1809 Callowhill St., Philadelphia, Pa. 19130.

WINDFALL PRESS, 1814-E Norwood St., Chicago, Ill.

THE WORLD PUBLISHING CO., 2231 West 110th St., Cleveland, Ohio 44102.

YOUNG PUBLICATIONS, 69 West Main St., Appalachia, Virginia 24216. Anthology publishers. No payment.

*SUBSIDY PUBLISHERS

DORRANCE & COMPANY, 1809 Callowhill St., Philadelphia, Pa. 19130.

EXPOSITION PRESS, 50 Jericho Turnpike,

Jericho, N. Y. 11753.

THE GOLDEN QUILL PRESS, Francestown, N. H. 03043.

PAGEANT PRESS, 101 Fifth Ave., New York, N. Y. 10003.

RUBERT PUBLICATIONS, 1110 Valley View Dr., Fayetteville, Ark.

VANTAGE PRESS, 120 West 31 St., New York, N. Y. 10001.

WILLIAM-FREDERICK PRESS, 55 East 86 St., New York, N. Y. 10028.

SUBMITTING GREETING CARD VERSE

The creation of salable greeting card verses is not easy. Some contributors are under the false impression that the publisher will buy "quickie" creations dashed off at odd moments. That attitude is completely erroneous. The extent of your success in selling original free lance material to the greeting card publishers will be in proportion to the amount of effort, talent, study and research that you put into the creation of your submissions.

Successful free lance writers who enjoy a steady sale of their original material in the greeting card field recognize the need for a strong combination of talent and hard work. They study greeting cards from every possible angle. They familiarize themselves with what is suitable and what is not suitable. They talk to friends and relatives about greeting cards. They talk to retailers about greeting card preferences expressed by customers. Through detailed research and by becoming fully familiar with all phases of greeting cards and the greeting card idea, they proceed carefully to create material that has some possibility of acceptance. They know it is useless to just dash off a few verses and send them in with the hope of getting an acceptance.

In recent years there have been so many submissions of totally unsuitable verses to the greeting card publishers that some are prone to give up in despair. They feel it is almost useless to spend the time and money required to inspect the vast amount of material they receive when so much of it is so carelessly written that it is totally unacceptable for greeting card use.

When submitting verse to greeting card publishers, send TYPEWRITTEN COPY ONLY. Use 3x5 or 4x6 cards or slips of paper. Type only one verse to a card. Type your name and address on the back of each card. Keep a careful record of all verses submitted, including date sent, date returned or accepted. Don't submit the same verses to more than one publisher at a time. Always include a stamped, self-addressed envelope bearing sufficient postage for the return of your verses by the publisher.

Remember that every successful greeting card must carry a message that involves a wish, a greeting, a compliment, or an expression of appreciation. Don't use words or figures of speech that you would not use in everyday conversation. Be original. Don't copy. Appropriation of another writer's original work is totally unethical. Direct or indirect copying or adapting of someone's verse may subject you to embarrassing and expensive legal action.

Most important of all—be honest with yourself. Before you submit anything to publishers, do everything possible to be sure that your material will stand up favorably in comparison with verses and ideas now being published on greeting cards. You can avoid a lot of disappointment and frustration if you will be fully objective in analyzing and appraising your own work.

*GREETING CARD VERSE PUBLISHERS

ALLIED PAPER, INC., 1151 W. Roscoe St., Chicago, Ill. 60657. Pays up to $50.00.

AMBERLEY GREETING CARD CO., 2835 Section Rd., Cincinnati, Ohio 45237. Pays $10.00 for each verse.

AMERICAN GREETINGS CORP., 1300 West 78th St., Cleveland, Ohio 44102.

BARKER GREETING CARD CO., 630 Burbank St., Cincinnati, Ohio 45206. Pays $15.00 to $35.00 for a verse.

SID J. BURGOYNE & SONS, INC., Allegheny Ave. at 22nd St., Philadelphia, Pa. 19132.

BUZZA-CARDOZO, 1500 S. Los Angeles St., Anaheim, Calif. 92803.

CALIFORNIA ARTIST, 311 Main St., Seal Beach, California.

CARD CRAFT CO., 33 - 34th St., Brooklyn, N. Y. 11232.

CASTLE LTD., % Kent Paper Co., Inc., 184 Kent Ave., Brooklyn, N. Y. 11211.

CENTURY ENGRAVING & EMBOSSING CO., 1020 West Adams St., Chicago, Ill. 60607.

CHARM CRAFT PUBLISHERS, INC., 33-35th St., Brooklyn, N. Y. 11232.

CURTIS CIRCULATION CO., Card Dept., Independence Sq., Philadelphia, Penn. 19105. Payment varies.

D. FORER AND CO., INC., 18 West 18th St., New York, N. Y. Pays $10.00 a verse.

THE DRAWING BOARD, P. O. Box 505, 1425 Dragon St., Dallas, Texas.

THE EXCLUSIVE CO., 901 West Glenwood Ave. Philadelphia, Pa. 19133.

FLAIR CARDS, INC., 550 West 58th St., New York, N. Y. 10019.

FRAN MAR GREETING CARDS, LTD., 110 East Third St., Mt. Vernon, N. Y. 10550. Pays $10.00 a verse.

FRAVESSI-LAMONT, INC., 11 Edison Place, Springfield, N. J.

GIBSON GREETING CARD, INC., 2100 Section Rd., Cincinnati, Ohio 45237. Pays $1.50 a line.

GRANT PUBLISHING CORP., 1050 West Fullerton Ave., Chicago, Ill. 60614.

GREENTREE PUBLISHERS, INC., 14-16 Greenbaum St., South Boston, Mass. 02127.

HALLMARK CARDS, INC., 25th & McGee, Kansas City, Mo. 64141. Pays $50.00 a verse.

HAMPTON GREETING CARD CO., 115 West Church St., Libertyville, Ill. 60048.

HAWTHORNE-SOMMERFIELD, INC., 100 Imlay St., Brooklyn, N. Y. 11231.

HINZ PUBLISHING CO., 1750 W. Central Rd., Mt. Prospect, Illinois.

HOUSE OF OZ, INC., 600 Getty Ave., Clifton, N. J. 07015. Pays $15.00 a verse.

KEEP 'N TOUCH, P. O. Box 212, Framingham, Mass. Pays $10.00 a verse.

ALFRED MAINZER, INC., 39-33 29th St., L. I., N. Y. 11101.

MILLER ART CO., INC., 70 Washington St., Brooklyn, N. Y. 11201.

MISTER B. GREETING CARD CO., 3500 N. W. 52nd St., Miami, Florida 33142. Payment varies.

MODERNE CARD CO., INC., 3855 Lincoln, Chicago, Ill. 60613. Pays $7.50 a verse.

THE NEWBURY GUILD, 76 Atherton St., Boston, Mass. 02130.

NOVO CARD PUBLISHERS, INC., 3855 Lincoln Ave., Chicago, Ill. 60613.

NU-ART ENGRAVING, 5823 N. Ravenwood Ave., Chicago, Ill. 60626.

PARAMOUNT LINE, INC., 400 Pine St., Pawtucket, Rhode Island.

RED FARM STUDIO, INC., Box 1239, Providence, Rhode Island.

REED STARLINE CARD CO., 3331 Sunset Blvd., Los Angeles, Calif. 90026.

THE ROSE CO., Bainbridge St. at 24th, Philadelphia, Pa. 19146.

NILE RUNNING STUDIO, 247 West 1st St., Claremont, Calif. 91711.

ROTH GREETING CARD, 6417 Selma Ave., Hollywood, Calif. 90028. Pays $15.00 for each verse.

RUST CRAFT GREETING CARDS, INC., Rust Craft Road, Dedham, Mass. 02026. Pays $1.25 a line.

SANGAMON, Taylorville, Illinois 62568.

SHOLOM GREETING CARD CO., INC., 26 South 6th Ave., Mt. Vernon, N.Y. 10550. Pays $15.00 for each verse.

E. ERRETT SMITH, INC., 141 East 25th St., N. Y., N. Y. 10010.

SUNSHINE ART STUDIOS, INC., 45 Warwick St., Springfield, Mass. Pays $1.50 a line.

TREASURE GREETINGS, 1575 Lake St., Elmira, N. Y. 14901.

UNITED CARD CO., 1101 Carnege St., Rolling Meadows, Illinois 60067. Pays $10.00 a verse.

VAGABOND CREATIONS, Box 94, West Carrolton, Ohio 45449. Pays $10.00 a verse.

WARNER PRESS PUBLISHERS, Fifth at Chestnut St., Anderson, Indiana 46011. Pays $1.00 a line.

WHITE CARD CO., 369 Congress St., Boston, Mass. 02110.

WILLIAMSBURG GREETINGS CORP., 3280 Broadway, New York, N. Y. 10027.

*FOREIGN MARKETS

(EDITOR'S NOTE: When submitting poems to foreign publishers, always enclose the customary self-addressed envelope, but DO NOT INCLUDE United States postage. Foreign publishers cannot use U. S. postage stamps in returning your material to you. Instead of stamps, send International Reply Coupons, which are available at most U. S. Post Offices. The publisher can exchange these IRC coupons for postage in his own country. For further information, ask your local postmaster.)

ACCENT, St. Luke's College, Exeter, Devon, U. K. Payment in contributors copies.

AGENDA, 5 Cranbourne Ct. , Albert Bridge Rd. , London SW, England. Payment in contributors copies.

AGENTZIA, 25 Rue Vandamme, Paris 14, France. Payment in contributors copies.

AGORA, JORNAL LITERARIO, Ave. 1 de Juhno 470, 2 Andar, sala 16, Divinopolis, Minas Gerais, Brazil. Payment in contributors copies.

AKROS, 14 Parklands Ave. , Penwortham, Preston, Lancashire, U.K. Pays 42s for each poem or page.

ALTA, 'Westmere', 50 Edgbaston Rd. , Birmingham 15, U.K.' Payment in contributors copies.

AMBIT, 17 Priory Gardens, London N. 6, U.K.
Payment varies.

AND, 262 Randolph Ave., London W. 9, U. K.
Payment in contributors copies.

ANGLO-WELSH REVIEW, 2 Croft Terr., Pem-
broke Dock, Wales. Payment in contributors
copies.

APLOMB, South St. Publications, 3 South St.,
Sherborne, Dorset, England.

APPROACHES, 11 Rue Cognacq Jay, Paris 7,
France. Payment in contributors copies.

ARCADE, 409 Liverpool Rd., London N. 7, England. Payment in contributors copies.

ARK, Royal College of Art, Exhibition Rd., S.
Kensington, London SW 7, U.K. Payment in contributors copies.

ARROWS, Students Union, Western Bank, Univ.
of Sheffield, Sheffield 10, England. Payment in
contributors copies.

ASOCIACION LITERARIA ARGENTINE, Carlos
Gardel 3185-1B, Buenos Aires, Argentina. Payment in contributors copies.

ASSASSINATORS BROADSHEET, 30 Effingham
Close, Sutton, Surrey, England. Payment in contributors copies.

ASYLUM, 478 Stanley Rd., Bootle, 20, Lancs, U. K.

THE ATLANTIC ADVOCATE, Phoenix Square, Fredericton, N.B., Canada.

AYLESFORD REVIEW, St. Alberts Press, Aylesford Priory, Nr. Maidstone, Kent, U.K.

B. B. BROOKS, 11 Clemantis St., Blackburn, Lancs, U.K. Pays with 20 contributors copies.

THE BEACON, 224 Great Portland St., London W. 1, England.

BLEW OINTMENT, 2270A W. 4th, Vancouver 9, B. C., Canada.

BO HEEM E UM, 3 South St., Sherborne, Dorset, England. Payment in contributors copies.

BOREAL, P. O. Box 262, Victoria Sta., Montreal 6, Canada.

BREAKTHRU, 38, Penn Crescent, Haywards Heath, Sussex, England.

BUST, 671 Spadina Ave., Toronto 4, Ontario, Canada. Payment in contributors copies.

CANADA CEMENT BULLETIN, Canada Cement Bldg., Phillips Square, Montreal, Quebec, Canada. Payment varies.

CANADIAN CHURCHMAN, 600 Jarvis St., Toronto 5, Ontario, Canada.

CANADIAN FORUM, 56 Esplanade St. E., Toronto 1, Ontario, Canada. Payment in contributors copies.

CANADIAN LIGHTS, Vanity Press, R. R. 4, Warkworth, Ont., Canada.

THE CANADIAN MESSENGER OF THE SACRED HEART, Box 100, Station G, Toronto 8, Ontario, Canada. Pays 50¢ a line.

CANADIAN POETRY, Box 2033, Station D, Ottawa, Canada.

CASTILE, Univ. College, Swansea, Wales.

CENTRAL LITERARY MAGAZINE, Oxford Univ. Press, 45 Sandhills Ln., Barnt Green, Worc., England.

CHATELAINE, 481 University Ave., Toronto 2, Ontario, Canada. Pays $5.00 to $25.00 for each poem.

CIRCUIT, 8 Chelmsford Sq., London NW 10, England.

CLA, Imprensa Universitaria do Ceara, Av. da Universidade 2932, Fortaleza, Ceara, Brazil.

CLARE MARKET REVIEW, London School of

Economics, **Students Union, London W. C. 2, England.** Payment in contributors copies.

COLLECTION, Flat 4, 7 St. Aubyns, Hove, Sussex, England. Payment in contributors copies.

COLLIER-MACMILLAN CANADA LTD., (Book publisher) 55 York St., Suite 1105, Toronto 1, Ont., Canada.

EL CORNO EMPLUMADO, Apt. Postal # 13-546, Mexico 13, D. F., Mexico. Payment in contributors copies.

THE COUNTRY GUIDE, 1760 Ellice Ave., Winnipeg 21, Manitoba, Canada. Pays 35¢ for each line.

THE CRITICAL QUARTERLY, Dept. of Eng., The University, Manchester, England. Payment varies.

CRUSADE, 30 Bedford Pl., London, W. C. 1, England.

DAMN YOU, 18 Hastings Rd., Allahabad-1 (U. P.) India. Payment in contributors copies.

365 DAYS OF THE YEAR, 92 Bromyard Rd., St. Johns, Worcs., U.K.

DE-COLLAGE, Typos Verlag, 6 Frankfurt, Grunebergweg 118, Germany.

DELTA, 12 Hardwick St., **Cambridge, England.**
Payment in contributors copies.

DELTA CANADA, (Book publisher) 3476 Ven-
dome Ave., Montreal, Quebec, Canada.

DOORWAY, 66 Northline Rd., Toronto 16, Ont.,
Canada. Pays $2.00 to $5.00 a poem.

THE DUBLIN MAGAZINE, Haccombe Parva,
Killiney Co., Dublin, Ireland. Payment in contributors copies or token.

ECO CONTEMPORANEO, Casila Correo Central
1933, Buenos Aires, Argentina. Payment in contributors copies.

EDGE, Box 4067, Edmonton, Alberta, Canada.
Payment in contributors copies.

EL CORNO EMPLUMADO, Apartado Postal #
13-546, Mexico 13, D. F., Mexico. Payment in
contributors copies.

EMBRYO, St. Anthony House, Oundle, Peterborough, U. K.

ENCOUNTER, 25 Haymarket, London, S. W. 1,
England. Payment varies.

ENCRES VIVES, 3 Rue de Verdun, Bram (Aude),
France.

ENIGMA, 18 Romford Rd., Pembury, Kent, U.K.

ENSAYO CULTURAL, Chacabuco 1291, 2, B, Buenos Aires, Argentina.

ENVOI, Seven Levels, Marle Hill Pde., Cheltenham, Glos., England. Pays 6s a poem plus contributors copies.

EXPRESSION, 56 Carlton Ave., Kenton, Harrow, Middlesex, England. Payment varies.

EZRA, Ezra-Fakir Press, 18, Allahabad (U.P.) India. Payment in contributors copies.

FAKIR, Ezra-Fakir Press, 18, Allahabad (U.P.) India. Payment in contributors copies.

FEVER, 69 Knighton Dr., Leicester, England.

THE FIDDLEHEAD, Dept. of English, U.N.B., Fredericton, N.B., Canada. Pays $5.00 for each poem.

THE FIELD, 8 Stratton St., London W. 1, England. Payment varies.

FIRE, 4 St. George's Terrace, London NW 1, England. Pays $12.00 for each page, plus contributors copies.

FIREFLOWER, Box 2170, Whitehorse, Yukon, Canada.

FISHPASTE II, 97 Holywell St., Oxford, England. Payment in contributors copies.

FITZHENRY & WHITESIDE, LTD., (Book publisher) 1590 Midland Ave., Scarborough, Ontario, Canada.

FLAME MAGAZINE, Univ. of Essex, Wivenhoe Park, Colchester, Essex, England.

FLEYE PRESS, 1431 Robson St., Vancouver 5, B.C., Canada. Payment in contributors copies.

FORGOTTEN DOORWAY, 2 Central Ave., Northfield, Birmingham 31, England. Payment in contributors copies.

FORM, 78 Norwich St., Cambridge, England. Payment in contributors copies.

FORTIFIED PRINACRIPTIONS, 49 Woodlawn Rd. London SW 6, U.K. Payment in contributors copies.

FRENTE, Rua Pouso Alegre, 295, Foresta, Belo Horizonte, Minas Gerais, Brazil.

GANDALF'S GARDEN, Love Ink, 10a Airlie Gdn. London W 8, England. Payment in contributors copies.

GROSSETESTE REVIEW, Grosseteste Press, 1 Stonefield Ave., Lincoln, U.K.

GRYPHON PRESS & MAINLINE, 166 Randolph Pl., Windsor, Ont., Canada.

GUINESS PUBLISHING, LTD., 111 Eglinton Ave. E., Toronto 12, Ont., Canada.

HAIKU, Box 866, Station F, Toronto, Ontario, Canada. Payment in contributors copies.

HARAVEC, Casilla 68, Miraflores, Lima, Peru. Payment in contributors copies.

HEINRICH HEINE PRESS, 10 Duncairn Rd., Don Mills, Ont., Canada.

THE HIBBERT JOURNAL, Manchester College, Oxford, England. Payment varies.

HUSTLER, 194 Westbourne Park Rd., London W 11, U.K.

HYPHID, 756 Bathurst St., Toronto 4, Ontario, Canada. Payment in contributors copies.

ICONOCLAST, 139 Elm Rd., New Malden, Surrey, U. K. Payment in contributors copies.

ICONOCLATRE, 71 Ryehill Gdns., Harlepool, Durham, U. K.

IMPRINT, Bridgewest Publ., 56 Harrow Rd., Bristol 4, U. K.

THE INFORMER INTERNATIONAL POETRY MAGAZINE, 16 Davenant Rd., Oxford, England. Payment in contributors copies.

INHERITED, 7 Evesham Rd., Cheltenham, Glos., England. Payment in contributors copies.

IN PARTICULAR, 97 Holywell St., Oxford, Eng. Payment in contributors copies.

INTERNATIONAL TIMES, 22 Betterton St., London WC 2, England. Pays with a subscription.

IS NOW, 65 Fairfield Rd., Kingston, Surrey, England. Payment in contributors copies.

JORNAL DE POESIA, Rua Carlos Fernandez 290, Hipodromo, Recife, Pernambuco, Brazil.

THE JOURNAL, Pioneer Press, Ruskin Bldgs. 191, Corporation St., Birmingham 4, England. Payment in contributors copies.

JUILLARD, 14 Wesley Rd., Leeds 12, England. Payment in contributors copies.

KING MOB ECHO, BCM/King Mob, London WC 1, United Kingdom.

LABRIS, Labyrinth Press, Sint-Hubertusstraat 54, Berchem-Antwerp.

LIBERTE, C.P. 97, Station H, Montreal, Can.

LINK, Gloucestershire Col. of Art, Pittville, Cheltenham, England. Payment in contributors copies.

LITTLE MOTHER OF BOL CANOES COLON PELLE, Pellebooks, 857 Sherbrook, # 12, Winnipeg 2, Manitoba, Canada. Payment in contributors copies.

LOUDSPEAKER, 27 Wilberforce Rd., Finsbury Pk., London N4, U. K.

LUV, 1431 Robson St., Vancouver, B. C., Canada.

THE MAGAZINE, 12 Carlton House Terrace, London SW 1, England. Payment in contributors copies.

MAINLINE, 179 Hanna E., Windsor, Ontario, Canada. Payment in contributors copies.

THE MALAHAT REVIEW, Univ. of Victoria, Victoria, B. C., Canada.

MANIFOLD, 99 Vera Ave., London N 21, England. Payment varies.

MANUSCRIPT, 45 Mayesbrook Rd., Dagenham, Essex, England. Payment in contributors copies.

McCLELLAND AND STEWART, LTD., (Book publisher) 25 Hollinger Rd., Toronto 16, Ontario, Canada.

MEANJIN QUARTERLY, University of Melbourne, Parkville N. 2, Victoria, Australia. Payment varies.

MESSAGE, 46 Rue Richer, Paris 9, France.

MINUS ONE, 2 Orsett Terrace, London W 2, England.

MODERN POETRY IN TRANSLATION, 10 Compayne Gdns., London NW 6, England. Payment varies.

MODERN WELSH PUBLICATIONS, Teify House, Abercynon, Mountain Ash, Flamorgan, Wales. Payment varies.

MOFUSSIL, 20 Hall Close, Kettering, Northants, U. K.

MOVEMENT, 9 Cornell, 84, Main Ave., Khar, Bombay 52, India. Payment in contributors copies.

NEBULUM'S OLIVE DACHSUND, Two Birds Press, % St. Peter's College, Oxford, England.

NOTHING DOING IN LONDON TWO, 10 Blacklands Terr., Sloane Sq., London SW 3, England.

OCTOPUS, 252 fg St. Honore, Paris 8, France.

OPEN LETTER, CSC Royal Roads, Victoria, B. C., Canada. Payment in contributors copies.

ORE, 11 High Plash, Stevenage, Herts, U. K.

OTHER VOICES, 1226 Richmond St., London,

Ontario, Canada. Payment in contributors copies.

OUTPOSTS, 209 East Dulwich Grove, London SE 22, England. Payment varies.

THE PARK, Dept. of Am. Studies, Keele Univ., N. Statts, England.

PEAU DE SERPENT, 15 Boulevard Lambermont, Bruxelles 3, Belgique.

PENTECOSTAL TESTIMONY, 10 Overlea Blvd., Toronto 17, Ontario, Canada. Pays $2.50 for each poem.

PHOENIX, Berlin 46, Strass 71 Nr 3, Germany.

PLATFORM, 117 Green Lane, West Vale, Halifax, Yorks, U. K.

POET, 4 A Motilal St., Madras 17, South India. Payment in contributors copies.

POET & PRINTER PRESS, 36 Halstead Rd., London E 11, England.

POETRY AND AUDIENCE, Leeds Univ. English Department, University Union, Leeds 2, England.

POETRY AUSTRALIA, 350 South Head Road, Five Dock, Sydney, N.S.W., Australia. Payment varies.

POETRY INDIA, The Retreat, Bellasis Road, Bombay 8 BC, India. Payment in contributors copies.

POETRY REVIEW, 21 Earls Court Square, London S. W. 5, England. Payment varies.

POETRY WORKSHOP, Wolverhampton Col. of Art, St. Peter's Close, Wolverhampton, Staff, England.

PORTO DE TODOS OS SANTOS, Rua Juliano Moreira, 11-5, and Sala 516, Salvador, Bahia, Brazil. Pays $6.50 a poem.

PRESBYTERIAN RECORD, 50 Wynwood Dr., Don Mills, Ontario, Canada. Payment varies.

PRIAPUS, 37 Lombardy Dr., Berkhamsted, Herts., England. Payment in contributors copies.

PRISM INTERNATIONAL, Department of Creative Writing, U. B. C., Vancouver 8, B. C., Canada. Payment varies.

PRISONER, 6-A/1B - Sector X, Bhilai, India.

PUBLICITY REVIEW, 104 Raleigh St., Alfreton Rd., Nottingham, England. Payment in contributors copies.

PUNCH, 10 Bouverie St., London E. C. 4, Eng.

QUARRY, Box 1061, Kingston, Ontario, Canada.

Payment in contributors copies.

QUEENS QUARTERLY, Room 524, Humanities Bldg., Queens University, Kingston, Ontario, Canada. Pays $3.00 a page.

QUILL, 2, The Drive, Mardleyhill, Welwyn, Herts, England. Payment in contributors copies.

REFUGEE JOURNAL OF POETRY, Box 28, Melifa, Manitoba, Canada. Payment in contributors copies.

RESURGENCE, 24 Abercorn Place, London NW 8, England.

RIDING WEST, 4 Nowell Place, Almondbury, Huddersfield, U. K.

RIVERSIDE QUARTERLY, Box 4C, University Station, Regina, Canada. Payment in contributors copies.

THE RYERSON PRESS, (Book publishers) 299 Queen St. W., Toronto 2B, Ontario, Canada.

SAMPHIRE, South Bank, Soring Rd., Ipswich, United Kingdom.

SATYRDAY, Box 12, 340 Bathurst St., Toronto 2B, Ontario, Canada. Payment in contributors copies.

SAUNDERS OF TORONTO LIMITED, (Book

publisher) 1885 Leslie St., Don Mills, Ontario, Canada.

SCRIP, 67 Hady Crescent, Chesterfield, Derbyshire, England. Payment in contributors copies.

THE SECOND AEON, 3 Maplewood Ct., Maplewood Ave., Llandaff North, Cardiff, Wales.

SOLSTICE, 21a Silver St., Cambridge, England. Payments pending.

SOMETHINGS, 32 Swindon Rd., Birmingham 17, United Kingdom.

SPANISH FLEYE, 1431 Robson St., Vancouver, B. C., Canada.

STANZA, 6 New Square, West Gorton, Manchester 12, United Kingdom.

STROPHIES, 9 Rue de Belfort, 92 Asneres, France. Payment varies.

STRUCTURE, 52, Queensway, London W2, Eng.

TAKE ONE, Box 1778, Station B, Montreal 2, P. Q., Canada.

TALON, 1911 Acadia Rd., Vancouver 8, B. C., Canada.

THE TAMARACK REVIEW, Box 159 Station K, Toronto 12, Ontario, Canada. Pays $10.00 for each page.

TAMARISK, 80 North Way, North Heath, Erith, Kent, United Kingdom. Awards.

TARASQUE, Trent Book Shop, Trent Bridge, Nottinghamshire, England. Payment in contributors copies.

TEEKKARI, Dipoli, Otaniemi, Finland.

TORNADO, Govindniwas, Sarojiniroad, Vile-Parle W., Bombay 56, India. Payment in contributors copies.

TOTAL, Munchener Strasse 26, 1, Berlin 62, W. Germany. Payment varies.

TRACKS, University of Warwick, Coventry, England (CV47AL) Payment in contributors copies.

TRANSFORMATION, 1, Deanery Place, Exeter, Devon, England.

UBULUM, St. Peter's College, Oxford, England. Payment in contributors copies.

UCL POETRY, UCL Poetry Seminar, London, Gower St., WC 1, England. Payment in contributors copies.

UNION FARMER, 333 4th Ave. North, Saskatoon, Sask., Canada. Pays 4¢ a word.

VANCOUVER LIFE MAGAZINE, 1012 Hornby St., Vancouver, B. C., Canada. Payment varies.

VIEWPOINTS, 20 Droylesden Rd., Newton Heath, Manchester 10, United Kingdom.

VOICE OF THE ELF*SELF, V.E.S. Enterprises, Box 1961, Wetaskiwin, Alberta, Canada.

WASCANA REVIEW, Wascana Parkway, Regina, Sask., Canada. Pays $10.00 a page.

WENDIGO, P. O. Box 1400, Sault Sainte Marie, Ontario, Canada. Payment in contributors copies and awards.

WEST COAST REVIEW, Simon Frazier University, Burnaby 2, B. C., Canada. Payment in contributors copies.

UNIVERSITY OF WINDSOR REVIEW, University of Windsor, Ontario, Canada. Payment in contributors copies.

WORKSHOP, 2 Culham Ct., Granville Rd., London N 4, England. Payment in contributors copies.

WRITERS FORUM POETS, 262 Randolph Ave., London W 9, England. Payment in contributors copies.

ZONA FRANCA, Apartado 8349, Caracas, Venezuela. Pays $20.00 to $25.00 a poem.

ANSWERS TO QUESTIONS

OFTEN ASKED BY POETS

Q. Should I copyright my poems before sending them to an editor?

A. No. Poems can't be copyrighted until AFTER they are published.

Q. If I must send the poems out without copyright, what is there to prevent an editor's using them without my permission and without any payment?

A. Your poems are protected at common law until they are published. No editor has a right to use your material without your permission. If he does, he is subject to both civil and criminal court action.

Q. If I submit poems to an editor who does not reply for several weeks, is it permissible to write and ask about them?

A. I would suggest you wait several months instead of weeks. The old adage, "No news is good news," applies here. If the editor is keeping your poems, there is every reason to believe he is still considering them for publication. If you write him too soon, he may return your poems at once just to quiet your anxiety.

Q. If I submit poems to an editor and haven't heard from him after six months, what should I do?

A. Write him a brief letter inquiring whether he received the poems, and whether he is considering them for publication. If you get no answer to the letter, write him another, stating that you are withdrawing the poems from his consideration. You may then send the poems to another publisher.

Q. Is it ethical to submit the same poems to several editors at the same time?
A. No. An editor will not consider your poems if he thinks they are being sent simultaneously to other editors. He wants exclusive use of the poems. If he learns that one of the poems he is considering has been accepted by another publication, he will return ALL your poems, and will remember this incident the next time you submit poems to him. Very likely, he will return all poems you send him in the future. Editors have long memories about things of this nature.

Q. When most editors reject poems, they send only a printed form rejection slip. Why don't they state the reasons for rejection?
A. An editor's job is to find publishable material. In some cases, his job is much more than that. He must lay out the magazine, deal with printers, write hundreds of letters, search for lost manuscripts, write advertising, and sometimes even sell the ads. Taking time out to comment on every poem submitted to him would be the equivalent of teaching a course in writing. It would be too time-consuming. Besides, many editors feel that beginners don't really appreciate any comments on their work—unless the

comments are favorable.

Q. How many submissions should I undertake before I give up on a particular poem?
A. Don't ever give up if you are convinced it is a good poem. Picking manuscripts is an intuitive business. What appeals to one editor does not necessarily impress the others. Some poems have been sent out as many as fifty times before finding acceptance.

Q. When should a poet submit holiday poems such as Christmas poems or Easter poems?
A. Submit them at least four months before the holiday arrives.

Q. When typing manuscripts, should I use pica or elite type?
A. Either is acceptable. Any typeface that is easy to read is satisfactory. Avoid the use of unusual typestyles such as script or all capital letters.

Q. I want to collect all my published poems and print them in book form. Must I get permission from the magazines in which they were published?
A. Yes, if the magazines were copyrighted. If they were NOT copyrighted, your poems may be reprinted by anyone—including yourself.

Q. Aren't all publications copyrighted?
A. No. Most weekly and daily newspapers are not copyrighted, although the syndicated material

they use is copyrighted by the syndicate. Many of the so-called "little" magazines are not copyrighted.

Q. How can I ascertain whether a publication is copyrighted?
A. Look for the copyright notice. In books, it is printed on either the title page or the reverse side of the title page. In magazines, it is usually printed on the contents page.

Q. What is a copyright notice?
A. A copyright notice consists of the word "copyright" and/or the symbol (c), the year of publication, and the name of the copyright owner. Example: Copyright (c) 1969 by Susan Scribe.

Q. I have had poems printed in our local newspaper, which is not copyrighted. Is there any way I can copyright these poems now?
A. No. When a poem is published in an uncopyrighted publication, it becomes public property and can be reprinted by anyone.

Q. Is there any way I can protect poems that I submit to an uncopyrighted publication in the future?
A. Yes. You can copyright them yourself. Ask the editor to print a copyright notice, using your name, immediately after the poem. Then write to the Register of Copyrights and ask for Form BB. Follow instructions in filling it out. This will cost you a fee of $6.00. Be sure each poem is worth that much to you before you decide to

do this. Consider, too, that some editors will be annoyed by this practice and will reject your poems altogether.

Q. What is the address of the Register of Copyrights?
A. Register of Copyrights, Library of Congress, Washington, D. C. 20540.

Q. How long is a copyright in effect?
A. A copyright secures protection for your work for a period of 28 years. It can then be renewed for another 28 years. After 56 years, the work is in the public domain.

Q. I want to have my poems published in book form. How do I go about copyrighting the book?
A. First, be sure that the copyright notice is printed in the book on either the title page or the verso of the title page. If the notice is printed elsewhere in the book, your copyright is lost and cannot be restored. Then write to the Register of Copyrights and ask for Form A. You must fill in Form A, and have it notarized. Return Form A to the Register of Copyrights along with two copies of the finished book, and a fee of $6.00. The Register will send your copyright certificate.

Q. What is the difference between a professional poet and an amateur?
A. Being a "professional" does not mean that a poet earns his living from writing poems. It means that his work is accepted in a wide variety

of publications.

Q. Is it possible to earn a living today by writing poems?

A. It may be possible, but not at all probable. Most poets make money by other methods. Carl Sandburg raised dairy goats and gave folk music concerts. Jesse Stuart teaches, lectures, writes novels, and operates a farm. Shakespeare made a living by writing poetry, but that poetry was in dramatic form and was presented on stage. Poets today don't earn much money direct from their poems. However, the prestige that comes with your acceptance as a poet can help you earn money from other sources.

Q. Is there any way I can be sure that ALL my poems will be published?

A. Yes. Publish them yourself. Most of the famous writers of today and yesteryear have published their own work at some time during their careers. Vachel Lindsay published a book titled "Poems to Trade for Bread" and tramped all over the country doing just that. Martin Pinkstaff, an Illinois poet, operates a service station. He also has his poems printed on sheets of paper and sells them to his customers for 10¢ each. Max Bodenheim, the Bohemian poet of Greenwich Village, would collar citizens on the street and say, "Look, you bourgeois swine, buy this book!" Walt Whitman printed his first edition of "Leaves of Grass," setting it up letter-by-letter in the printshop of a friend.

Q. How do I go about publishing my own work?

A. Some poets have their poems printed in book form and simply give the books to their friends, associates, club members, etc. If you want to sell your books, you can learn how the pros do it by reading books on publishing. Your public library probably has several you should read. The following three titles contain much valuable practical information, and may be ordered direct from their respective publishers:

WHAT HAPPENS IN BOOK PUBLISHING by Chandler B. Grannis. Columbia University Press, 440 W. 110 St. N. Y., N. Y. 10025. $8.50.

A GUIDE TO BOOK-PUBLISHING by Datus C. Smith, Jr. R. R. Bowker Co., 1180 Avenue of the Americas, N. Y., N. Y. 10036. $6.00.

HOW TO PUBLISH YOUR BOOK by Lincoln B. Young. Young Publications, 69 W. Main St., Appalachia, Virginia 24216. $2.00.

Q. What are the addresses of some writer's magazines that poets should read?

A. THE WRITER, 8 Arlington St., Boston, Mass. 02116. Subscription $5.00. Sample 50¢.

WRITER'S DIGEST, 22 E. 12th St., Cincinnati, Ohio 45210. Subscription $4.00. Sample 50¢.

AUTHOR & JOURNALIST, Suite 870 National Press Bldg., Washington, D. C. 20004. Subscription $6.00. Sample $1.00.

SMALL PRESS REVIEW, Box 123, El Cerrito, California 94530. Subscription $3.50. Sample $1.00.

Q. Is there a special postal rate for manuscripts

and books?

A. Yes. Current rate is 12¢ for the first pound, and 6¢ for each additional pound. To be eligible for this rate, your package must be marked, "Special Fourth Class Rate: Manuscript," or "Special Fourth Class Rate: Books," whichever is the case. If a letter is enclosed in the package you must pay an extra 6¢ for the letter. As you know, postal rates and regulations change frequently. Inquire at your post office before mailing at these rates.

SELLING YOUR SONGPOEM

There are several firms around the country that prey on amateur lyricists and would-be songwriters. Most of them are located in the music centers of the nation—Hollywood, New York, and Nashville. You have seen their advertisements in various magazines. Their appeals run similar to this:

SONGPOEMS WANTED to be set to music. Our competent staff of composers and arrangers can expertly prepare your songpoem for professional presentation to RECORD COMPANIES and MUSIC PUBLISHERS. Examination, advice, and information absolutely FREE! Send your best poems to: SUCKER SONG SERVICE, Box 000, Hollywood, California.

These people are the charlatans of the music business. They are known by the Better Business Bureau as "song sharks." They are geniuses of a sort. Their genius lies not in composing a suitable melody for your "song," but in the clever methods they have devised for raiding the billfolds and bank accounts of unsuspecting amateur poets. They have no connections with the legitimate world of music. Real music publishers and record companies shun them like a fatal epidemic. So should you.

If you want proof, try this: Write a song lyric about any subject that comes to mind. Make it as ridiculous and inane as possible. Send a copy to each of the firms that advertise for songpoems. Without exception, you will receive a reply from each of them. Along with booklets, brochures and fake testimonials, you will get a form letter proclaiming the "exceptional quality" of your lyric and the "definite talent" they have discerned from the sample of your work. Now for a fee of "only" $60.00, they will be happy to have one of their "well-known composers" write the music and prepare your song for presentation to music publishers, record companies, vocalists, radio and TV, motion picture companies, eminent bandleaders, etc., etc.

Sounds lovely, doesn't it? Okay, go ahead and send them the $60.00. That's what you want to do, isn't it? (You and thousands of others before you.) They'll fit a melody to your poem all right. There is one thing these fellows can do besides write irresistible advertising material, and that is write melodies. They can steal a bar here, a bar there, and whip up a melody before you can say Rodgers and Hammerstein. It may be a lilting melody for your melancholy poem; it may be a plaintive melody for your jubilant poem; it most certainly will be a less-than-mediocre melody, but it WILL be a melody.

In exchange for your $60.00 they will send you TWO whole copies of your song complete with copyright in YOUR NAME. The copyright costs the song shark the tremendous sum of $6.00. That leaves $52.00 for your two copies of your song. Only $26.00 per copy. Well, now, that's not so bad, is it?

Along with these two lead sheets of your song comes the next sales pitch. For only $60.00 more the Song Service will make up and print several hundred "piano copies" of your song. After all, these piano copies are necessary, they tell you, if you want your song presented properly to music publishers, vocalists, record companies, etc.

You can't stop now while victory is almost in sight. You will send them another $60.00. They will print the piano arrangements and will mail them to publishers, etc., along with hundreds of other piano arrangements from hundreds of other hopefuls like yourself. When these bundles of amateur songs arrive at the publisher's office, they are either returned unopened or are quickly consigned to the wastepaper basket as soon as the secretary sees the name of the firm from which they came. But there is no cause for you to bewail the loss of your $120.00. All the man at Song Service promised was to write a melody, print copies, and present (mail) them to publishers, record companies, etc. And he did just that.

In the meantime you will receive more form letters from your "collaborator." He will reiterate his great faith in your song and the probability of its becoming a "smash hit." But a song as excellent as yours should have an additional amount of promotion to assure it the attention it deserves. A "demonstration record" would be just the thing. Your "friend" will be glad to press not less than 100 demonstration records, of which he will send you five and will "present" the other ninety-five to executives of recording companies. Your cost is "only" $250.00 for the 100 records on which your song will be sung by a "well-known" recording artist who makes demonstration records only as a sideline. There will be piano accompaniment of course. But if you would prefer a five-piece band for accompaniment, he will manage that, too, for only $150.00 more. And it will make your record more presentable.

The demonstration records, when received by the legitimate publishers and recording companies, meet the same fate as your printed piano arrangements. But you don't know this because no one ever tells you—certainly not your "collaborator."

After a year or so of listening for your song on the radio and TV, looking for it on juke boxes and in music stores, and waiting for the contract from the motion picture companies, you will begin to feel discouraged. You will write to your "collaborator" and inquire about your song. He will tell you that "some songs just don't click even though they have all the qualities necessary to make the top ten. Now if you have another good lyric, perhaps one that is just a little better than the last one, we will be glad to set it to music," etc., etc., ad nauseam.

This situation could continue forever. It is limited only by (1) your good sense, (2) the amount of your life's savings, or (3) the shark's imagination.

So many rackets have been worked in the songwriting field that the American Society of

Composers, Authors and Publishers, which is probably the best authority on song publishing, has issued a list of "Don'ts for Songwriters." They say:

"Don't pay anybody to set your words to music. Write your own melody or collaborate with a melody writer who will gamble his talent with yours. Don't pay any publisher to publish your song, or for any other service whereby the publisher promises publication. Reliable publishers pay all costs of publishing and pay you a royalty.

"Don't listen to any concern or individual who tells you that songwriting is an easy road to fame and fortune, or who praises your work unduly and sends you literature telling about the fortunes other writers have made from their songs. Don't accept any of the so-called "50—50 collaborations" whereby you are called upon by your collaborator to pay him a fee for one service or another, no matter how enticing they may sound. Such composers accept your fee and leave you holding the sack, making their profit on the money you pay to them, no matter how small."

If you aspire to be a songwriter you must take songwriting seriously. You must have more than normal talent, and you must know something about music. Preferably, you should be capable of playing some musical instrument, and have the ability to compose your own melodies to complement your particular lyrics. At least you must be well acquainted with someone who can write the melodies. Song sharks are interested only in the fees you pay them, and will give you very little in return.

Let's assume that you have written a lyric and have an appropriate melody in mind. If you can hum or sing the melody you should be able to find someone locally who can put the notes on paper for you. Perhaps it will be a local music teacher, or a high school band director. When you have the words and music written down on paper, any offset printer can photograph and reproduce a thousand copies at a cost of only ten to twenty dollars.

It is true that you will need demonstration records made of your song. But don't trust this to the song sharks. Hire a local band to play the song, and get a good singer to sing it. Then have a tape recording made.

There are several firms that specialize in making demo records from your tape. You can find their names and addresses in the musical trade magazines. Contact some of them and compare their products and prices. Send your tape recording to one of them and have several demo records made. They will do a better job for less money than the song sharks.

With your printed sheet music and your demo records in your possession, you must now emigrate to one of the nation's music centers. If country and western music, or gospel music, is your forte, head for Nashville. If your song is of a more general nature, go to Hollywood or New York. Songwriting can't be done by mail from your home by submitting song sheets and records to music publishers the way you submit poems to magazine editors. Music publishers don't want to receive unsolicited songs from non-professional songwriters. They are too busy evading the novices in their own offices.

If you are concerned about someone stealing your song, you'd better have it copyrighted before you leave home. To do this, write to the Register of Copyrights, Library of Congress, Washington, D. C. 20540. Ask for Form E. When it arrives, follow the instructions in filling it out.

Now comes the wearisome, discouraging, mundane process of trudging from door to door of the music publishers. Most of them will try to avoid you, especially the larger publishers. The receptionist has her orders. She will tell you one of several things: (a) the firm has its own staff of writers and accepts no "outside" songs; (b) the publisher is not interviewing composers at present; (c) there is no one in the office at the moment to listen to your song. In the event the publisher does come out to greet you, he will state that his catalogue is filled up until spring (if it is fall) and vice versa if it is spring. This is just his diplomatic way of saying that he wants no part of you or your song.

After several such encounters you will be asking yourself, "What's wrong with these s.o.b.s? Don't they want to publish any songs?"

But stop and think for a minute. A publisher must invest many thousands of dollars in promoting a song. For that reason he must have great enthusiasm for your song before he will take the risk. He knows, too, that it takes years for a person with plenty of talent to master the art of songwriting. You are an unknown quantity to him. He is no more likely to risk his time and money on you than he will permit himself to be operated on by an amateur surgeon, or deposit his life's savings with an amateur banker.

Let's say that you are lucky. You have found a publisher who at least will listen to your song. Probably he will be a small publisher who hasn't many hits behind him, if any. He will escort you into his private office, place your record on his phonograph, and listen. Chances are he will say, "No, it's not for us." But if you are lucky again, he might scratch his head and ask you to leave it for further consideration. What can you lose? Leave it. Naturally you have several other demonstration records. In the meantime you can try to present them to the executives of other publishing houses.

Maybe somewhere along the way you will find a publisher who takes an active interest in your song. And maybe not. It is difficult to approach publishers when you yourself are unknown. One famous songwriter had to break a window with a cobblestone to get recognition. (We don't recommend this method.) Another dropped a handful of pennies when the publisher passed near him. Others have taken jobs in publishing houses in any capacity, regardless of the amount of pay, just to get acquainted with the elite of the music world. Knowing the right people helps tremendously.

But suppose you have made the rounds of all

the publishing houses and no one shows any interest in your song. You don't want to go to jail for breaking windows. You are unwilling or unable to take a minor job with a publisher. You have no acquaintances among the select inner circle. What then?

You have one alternative. Approach the recording artist direct. The best time to do this is when he is on the road, playing engagements at theatres, ballrooms, and nightclubs throughout the country. You might gain access to him backstage before the show, or you might have to stand in line along with fans seeking autographs. Either way, you will have time to tell him about your song, and give him one of your demo records and a printed copy of the words and music. Be sure your name and address is on each so he can contact you if he likes the song.

Do this with every recording artist who, in your opinion, might want to add the song to his repertoire. If one of them likes the song well enough, he will sing it before an audience. If the audience responds favorably, he will obtain your permission to record it. In the meantime, all you can do is wait and hope, while writing other songs.

Songwriting is a hard field to enter. It is not recommended to the faint of heart. You must have real talent, and have faith in that talent. Otherwise you will not survive the continuous disappointments, heartaches, and all the other torments that are part of the profession. Remember, too, that songwriting requires an investment. You must have money to get your songs printed and to have demonstration records made. And money to sustain you while you try to get your songs published. If you don't have these qualities and resources, better forget it. There are easier and surer ways to earn a livelihood.

NOTE TO READERS

This handbook contains the most comprehensive list of poetry markets in print. At the time this list was compiled, it was accurate. It is well known, however, that publishers as well as other organizations sometimes change their address, change their policies, have business failures, or go into some other field of endeavor. For this reason, keeping a market list completely current is an impossible task.

We will maintain a list that is as up-to-date as possible by reprinting this directory at least once each year. To do this, we need your help. If in seeking a market for your poems you find that a publisher has discontinued publication, changed his address, or no longer uses poetry, we would appreciate your informing us to that effect. We can then make the correction in our next edition.

There is another way, too, that you can help us as well as other poets. If you know of any publication or radio or TV program that is not listed here, but which accepts poems from free lance writers, please let us know.

In our next edition we would like to list all poetry groups, federations, organizations, etc. If you belong to any kind of poetry group, regardless how small, please send information about it. To anyone submitting any usable information or ideas that will help us to publish a better edition of the POET'S HANDBOOK, we will send a complimentary copy of the next edition.

Jeanne Hollyfield, Editor

Poets have a license to lie.
—Pliny, The Younger

The poetry of earth is never dead.
—John Keats

Every man is a poet when he is in love.
—Plato

Truth shines the brighter clad in verse.
—Alexander Pope

All men are poets at heart.
—Ralph Waldo Emerson

DATE DUE

FEB 17 '71			
RESERVE			
MAY 8 '74			
JE 20 '80			
GAYLORD			PRINTED IN U.S.A.